ART FUNDAMENTALS

ART FUNDAMENTALS
THEORY AND PRACTICE

Second Edition
by
Otto G. Ocvirk
Robert O. Bone
Robert E. Stinson
Philip R. Wigg

School of Art / Bowling Green University
Bowling Green, Ohio

WM. C. BROWN COMPANY, PUBLISHERS / DUBUQUE, IOWA

FOREWORD

A worthwhile book is always written out of an assumed need and on the basis of what it intends to do about it. A book on art instruction, perhaps more than any other kind, should be equally realistic about what it cannot do. Beyond a certain point, the more one attempts to be "systematic" in this instruction, the more one misses the essential value of art. One cannot legislate feelings or emotions, and art is nothing if it lacks these qualities. One cannot prescribe personality, and art is always stamped with the honest imprint of its author.

Art instruction, therefore, narrows down to a few simple procedures which are deceptively complex in their application. It always succeeds or fails with the sensitivity of the student and his capacity for work. A person who would teach art well must learn to live with the knowledge that this student sensitivity feeds on the enthusiasm exhibited by the teacher. An atmosphere of creative excitement is always the most important step toward meaningful art instruction.

Beyond this, instruction in art must function elastically; it should always be presented on as personal a basis as possible, but it should also insure that personal experiences add up to those factors which are fundamental in art expression. In short, there should be some system to the instruction but the "system" should be kept within tolerances which permit discovery. There must always be a point at which the student may take over.

This book is an effort to fulfill the need for such a cautious system of instruction. It is not a "How-to-do-it" book; it contains no rules, formulas, or guarantees. In art such things are not possible; it is, however, predicated on certain principles which are presumed to be of such a fundamental nature as to encompass a wide range of expression. These principles are those which underlie every work of art, historical and contemporary, and can hardly claim to be original with the authors. Their search was not for novelty but for a sound but supple method of guidance which will encourage the development of understanding and ability. One should always be aware that most of the original thinking in this field is in the art, not on it.

Thinking and feeling are the two prerequisites to the successful use of the problems in this book; they are meant to be sensed and understood, not mechanically repeated. None of the problems, individually, is of any great importance, nor is the resultant work likely to be of surpassing beauty. But each exercise represents a problem which eventually appears in the total art form. Once the problem has been experienced, it is easier to recognize it as such and find its answer.

The best use of the recommended creative exercises can be made only if the text has been read before and after their execution. If the work is being done in a class, the chapters may very well serve as a basis for lecture and/or discussion. Text presentation has been deliberately kept at a reasonably challenging level (despite the fact that the book deals with the elementary phases of art) in the belief that this approach provides stimulation for a greater range of abilities.

Organization on the basis of art elements is a method which evolved out of the instructional experiences of the authors. Any book on art must break down *form* in some way in order to illustrate and instruct, and division into the elements of art structure of *line, shape, value, texture,* and *color* has the advantage that these elements, universal and unchanging, are unlikely to be challenged in their interpretation. The one disadvantage of this division is the one which is recognized as being a potential threat in any course of study— the possibility that the student may fail to make a final integration of the concepts illustrated by this breakdown. If an instructor is present, it is his responsibility to see that any learning developing out of the study of any *one* art element should find application in any future work.

The use of this book should be accompanied by studies of reproductions, and, even more, of original works of art. No text of this kind is able to provide ample quantity and quality of illustration. Those which were here selected were chosen because they were considered the most obvious examples of points brought up in the text. Most of them are good works of art, but certainly not of uniformly high quality in everyone's judgment. Their use here does not suggest a sweeping endorsement of their value. One of the interesting things about art is that there is rarely, if ever, an art work which is wholly good or wholly bad. An illustration used to depict an admirable quality of one sort might very well be used to show an unfortunate lapse in some other respect. Use the pictures with discrimination and judgment or even as the focus of healthy debate.

Terminology is included in the book solely for the establishment of a common basis of communication between those using it. It is impossible to find universal agreement among art people on terms, their significance, or their interpretation. A glance at other art books will confirm that words, definitions, and emphases vary. Consistency seems to be the important thing here; use of the book will be more profitable if its vocabulary is used consistently. It has been said that Georges Braque once remarked that he wanted his students to paint in his style as long as they studied with him; only in this way did he feel that they could understand each other. Anyone who has taught art understands the wisdom and the danger in this remark; but the danger is avoided if the "style" or "method" is understood as being only a temporary expedient. In a sense, this book may be considered a "temporary expedient." It is *temporary* in the sense that anyone who would become an artist must go far beyond it; it is *expedient* because it is hoped that its composition will expedite the development of sound attitudes.

ACKNOWLEDGMENTS

Every author has his share of "silent" partners, and only he can know how silent he himself would be if deprived of their support. As one thinks back on this group its numbers continue to grow, as well as one's sense of indebtedness and humility. It seems somewhat ungracious to consign these helpers to the semi-anonymity for which this page is traditionally intended. But it may be some consolation to our silent co-conspirators to know they are exonerated of any risk to which our writing may expose them.

The chief beneficiaries of our gratitude are two great repositories of art, The Museum of Modern Art, of New York, and The National Gallery, of Washington, D.C. Collectively they have supplied the bulk of the works newly reproduced in this edition. Their cooperative indulgence has been immeasurably helpful.

Most readers are not aware that this book has served as the basis of a television series on Art Fundamentals for Bowling Green University students. The televising of this course has given us a new insight into the book which, we think, has been reflected in the preparation of this second edition. Credit for this must go to Donald Ungurait, the enthusiastic and perceptive director.

Willard Wankelman gave the first edition its initial momentum, and has been unsparing with the spurs in the preparation of this material. As a beneficial irritant he is unsurpassed.

Finally, our wives have again endured our abdication from the family, thus adding to their already impressive credentials for sanctification.

CONTENTS

LIST OF BLACK AND WHITE ILLUSTRATIONS

LIST OF COLOR ILLUSTRATIONS

ART FUNDAMENTALS

CHAPTER 1: INTRODUCTION

One of the familiar characteristics of our times is ceaseless and often violent change. The promise and threat of this change is sensed by us all. We sometimes wish we could make time stand still, so that we could experience the comfort and security that we think might come with absolute values, standards by which we could with certainty, isolate the good from the bad. Yet, in so wishing we know that we delude ourselves; we all, as human beings, share in the desire for "progress." Few, if any of us, would be content to revert to the discomforts of an earlier age, and none of us would be happy to live in that age if it meant the surrender of our individuality. It is this individuality which produces everything on which we place any value, which creates progress—in short, change. If we are to honor individuality we must honor its expression; this is often easy to do when expression comes in the form of a product clearly usable. It is not so easy for us to value expression in its pure form as art, particularly when, in this form, individuality is undisguised and speaking as it must, in many ways.

Since change is such an obvious factor in our society, and since this is magnified in art by the search for individual expression, the newcomer to art may ask if there is any genuinely reliable standard which can guide him through the hazards of shifting historical styles and seemingly contradictory theories. The less diligent of us might be content to stand pat in so far as art matters are concerned; indeed, this may seem the easiest path although in the end, the least satisfying. It is always easier to argue against things than to learn what they are all about. Any learning (or expansion of outlook) calls for a discard of old and comfortable standards, a sacrifice which, in art frequently involves many of our cherished opinions. The learner in art must be willing to concede the possible validity of the many unfamiliar forms of individual expression; this means that the learner must place his own taste on trial.

We cannot deny that personal taste is always influential in forming art judgments, but we would certainly be remiss in not investigating the origins of this taste. Personal preference without benefit of experience cannot legitimately pose as criticism in art or any other field. We may argue our feelings by saying that "one man's meat is another man's poison," but, in saying this, we must remember that this cliché deals with exceptions to the rule. In *general* meat is nourishing and poison is quite the opposite; so that, although individual reactions may vary, there is still an essential difference between meat and poison as far as most of us are concerned. In art one may say "that's bad" or "that's good," but it is prudent to question whether one is speaking from the standpoint of purely personal reaction and, if so, whether this constitutes an acceptable evaluation. If the critic is seriously pressed on this point, he is less likely to make snap judgments.

Why must our immediate reaction to a work of art be regarded with suspicion? In making a decision, one invariably calls into play all those past experiences which might have any relationship to the problem at hand. Whether we like it or not, these experiences cannot be translated into concrete, verifiable material in the field of art. An engineer, on the contrary, faced with a professional problem in building a bridge, is able to convert experience into mathematical forms which can furnish proof. On the other hand, a problem in art judgment which is compounded of feelings and understanding is less factual and more general in its nature. The solution therefore lies, in a large part, with our intuition. This does not mean that a decision cannot be justified, but it does mean that the defense is more difficult than the prosecution. The novice in art, lacking the benefit of experience, has no course than to let his feelings rule his judgment. Lacking a basis for comparison and evaluation, he is frequently led out on a limb. His opinion forms in a twinkling, instinctively; the concepts produced by his limited background quickly jell into positive or negative attitudes.

In view of the subconscious nature of the art experience, our critic might find some difficulty in accounting for his seemingly automatic reactions. He could say that a work is "pretty," but what does that say, and must that be the end of the argument? Is the "prettiness" incapable of description or analysis? Are there principles by means of which this elusive quality can be argued or illustrated, or must the sensation of prettiness be confined to the individual observer? He may say that the work reminds him of something within his memory which was pleasurable, but this would seem to indicate that the beauty was not available to those lacking the advantage of the experience by which the work was judged. Does this mean that the quality of a work varies according to the person viewing it; or is it possible that there are qualities which could make it meaningful to people having little in common?

These are some of the disturbing questions which can arise when one becomes aware that passive acceptance of inherited attitudes can thwart new experience and understanding. By taking things for granted, by failing to realize that art necessarily takes many forms, one erects a screen, the fixed concept or petrified viewpoint, which seals off its enjoyment. The solidified concept develops steadily and frequently unconsciously; for instance, once accustomed to an environment, we perform our duties with a regularity which, in time, becomes automatic routine. The pattern of such activities soon is taken for granted to the extent that it may become a real discovery to find that others may have an entirely different approach to the same tasks. Our standards of morality similarly become "built in." We are sometimes shocked to find that moral codes in other societies frequently contradict our own. It would take little effort however to establish that, in the long run, evolving economies and human relationships result in gradual but very definite moral changes in our own culture. As an example, we need only mention the contrast between mid-Victorian and contemporary attitudes.

Art expression also changes steadily according to traceable reasons, but it is often more difficult to understand because we do not live consciously with art as we do with the restraints of society. Unless art changes with the times it loses most of its meaning, for it exists only to reflect us and our opinions of the world. Unfortunately, for many of us, taste in art undergoes no evolution but remains where it was when we received our first (too often least or last) exposure to art as a child, at the height of our formative period, through the taste of our parents, the environment of the school room, and the general preferences of the times. From this point on, our idea of art is likely to undergo little revision, unless an extraordinary interest in the subject motivates us toward more active observation or participation. True, we are often confronted with advertising and illustrational art, but such work is usually limited by the necessity of its commercial applications.

In view of the foregoing, it is little wonder that confusion, embarrassment, or defiance is often exhibited in face of a serious work. Genuine art is unlimited in its modes of expression; it sells no product but its own quality; it tells no obvious story but inclines one toward general attitudes of thought; it exhibits its art elements simply for the excitement their relationships afford; it does not limit itself to superficial appearances but tries to reveal that which lies deeper; and, it takes delight in pure adventure and invention.

If we further examine these characteristics of serious art, we discover that basically they are nonpractical in nature and obviously ask us to divorce ourselves from practical matters in order to enjoy them. In an age of automation and technical emphasis, it is difficult to imagine anything as an end in itself rather than a means to an end. This, however, was our childhood view of things; as a child, we were surprised and delighted by those things which we now think of as commonplace in life. We were not at all concerned with the functions of the objects we encountered but enjoyed them as things unique and marvelous in their own right. Our concepts were not fixed but constantly developing, and every moment of life was an adventure. The true art enthusiast must recapture some of this impractical awe in order to make art meaningful to him. He must remind himself that we do not enjoy a sunset by counting dust particles and measuring light rays; that indeed a scientist's factual description of a sunset would forfeit much of the beauty found in a poetic description, a beauty found in eloquence, selectivity, and exaggeration.

Thus we see that, whereas facts may play a part in art, there is really little excuse for judging a work of art purely on the basis of accuracy. One would probably be willing to concede that a true-false examination would be a poor basis for the grading of a painting; a more effective evaluation would be a review of its effects on one's private feelings. When an artist works, he is moved by impressions rather than specific things. The artist's reaction is general rather than precise, and to judge his product by any other standard is to miss his intentions. The true critic is also affected more by impression than by fact; if he saw an area of green on a canvas, he would not immediately concern himself with its identification as trees, grass, or water, but would be much more interested in the emotional feelings provoked by that particular green in its interplay with the other color areas.

The growth of understanding and enjoyment is possible in art, as it is in other fields, *provided* the individual has the interest and resolution to make full use of his powers of observation and introspection. It is foolish to speak of the artistic to one who has no ambition for sensing it, nor any intention of taking the time to view works of art again and again. The faculties of judgment must be enlarged and kept fresh by constant practice. Happily, the opportunities for this practice present themselves every day. Art infiltrates every phase of life; we must often choose wallpaper, carpeting, interior and exterior color, and all the other fixtures and furnishings which play a part in our domestic environments. Our choice is generally made on the basis of whatever feeling we have for the principles of design, and we may sometimes feel frustration because we know that our selective faculties have lain dormant, undeveloped by any of the educative processes by which we have developed our capabilities in other areas.

Fundamentally, the principles through which we design and furnish our homes are the very ones which underlie all phases of creative expression. The more closely we can keep to an open recognition of these principles the more sound will be the style created by our discrimination. The terms "fad" and "fashion" refer to temporary trends which are misapplications or misinterpretations of the underlying nature of design, but "style" in the best sense of the word refers to a quality which is enduring because it is not icing on the cake, but the cake itself. No doubt all of us have at times become nearsighted victims of fashions or fads whose extreme popularity while in vogue aid their infiltration into the intimacies of our lives. Yet, given the perspective of a few years, we may be appalled to find that the presumed stylishness was, in fact, a breach of good taste. The garish and synthetic character of many of the fashions of the twenties, for example, is obvious to most of us now, but the delusion of the people of that time was virtually complete, much to our current amusement.

Art, being human in its origin, has never been exempt from the dictates of fashion. It was nonconformity to fashion which led his contemporaries, and indeed people for many years later, to overlook Rembrandt as a significant artist. It was the fashionableness of devotion to classical art which for centuries caused men to classify art of the medieval period as "Gothic" or barbaric. Our own private fixation of concept is but a faint reflection of the paralysis of vision which may affect cultures and populations for generations. Of course, one cannot and should not shut his eyes to the present nor fail to be a part of it. But it is possible to develop a vision which looks through the encrustations of fashion, fad, and temporary prejudice into the bone and marrow of formal structure which is the ultimate gauge of soundness in art. Genuine quality does not, therefore, necessarily subtend popular or personal bias. The minor roots of art are imbedded in temporary preference, but the fundamental roots are those which force down through all eras of art and their attendant phraseologies.

We could, for want of a better term, call these formal roots the "Core of Universality" in this book because attention to form epitomizes those art products which survive time through generations of fluctuating taste. Form is also universal in the sense that it rises above geographical boundaries, and makes the works of various cultures meaningful to each other despite the fact that they may be largely alien in other respects. We may consider ourselves fortunate that we are living in an age which, through research and widespread reproductions, makes the output of all the peoples of the earth, past and present, accessible to us. This puts us in a favorable position to detect the common qualities of those works of art which have retained their significance. Invariably the same qualities

are detectable, although they are, as would be expected in works of any depth, difficult to analyze or describe.

The development of the formal qualities of a work of art takes place in the feelings of the artist, and it is only through the use of our feelings that we are able to perceive them. Perception or intuition can be sharpened and refined by an explanation of the principles of pictorial organization and, even more, by practice in their use. Ideally this practice is sought through exercises of increasing ambition (as in this book), and through constant and critical probing of the works of art of all historical periods. Some gifted individuals possess an inherent responsiveness to form which may shorten this educative process, or even render it unnecessary. But most of us can best find this new vision when our interest is tied to some systematic method of search and guidance. This is true because the fundamental properties of art are those which are most effectively concealed from the inexperienced observer; in fact, many beginning art students are highly skeptical of the existence of some of the things which the instructor may read into works of art. This is not surprising; the experience always lies *within* the observer, and the instructor has no tangible evidence of its presence except by developing the insight of his students. In this sense, art could be compared to religion—faith must often come before understanding. If the beginner is willing to accept, on faith, some of the basic premises of this book, an enlarged understanding of the nature of art should be expected. This should not be interpreted as saying that this understanding will be final, or that an artist will be created; artists are those who learn to make use of their growing understanding through trial and error. As soon as they begin to feel that they know everything about art, they cease to be *artists*. Mistakes are to be expected in art as in any learning process; it is the eventual *recognition of error* which guarantees development, and recognition occurs only at the highest intensity of one's thoughts and feelings.

CHAPTER 2: THE NATURE OF ART

Definitions:

Media, mediums: The materials and tools used by the artist to create the visual elements perceived by the viewer of the work of art.

Technique: The manner and skill with which the artist employs his tools and materials to achieve a predetermined expressive effect. The ways of using the media can have an effect on the aesthetic quality of the artist's total concept.

Style: The specific artistic character and dominant form trends noted in art movements or during specific periods of history. It also may mean the artist's expressive use of the media to give his work an individual character.

Craftsmanship: Aptitude, skill, or manual dexterity in the use of tools and materials.

Representation: A manner of expression by the artist in which the subject matter is naturalistically presented so that the visual elements seen by the observer are reminiscent of actual forms previously perceived.

Optical perception: A way of seeing in which the mind seems to have no other function than the natural one of providing the physical sensation of recognition of form.

Naturalism: The approach to art in which all forms used by the artist are essentially descriptive representation of things visually experienced. True naturalism contains no interpretation introduced by the artist for expressive purposes.

Abstract, abstraction: A term given to forms created by the artist but usually derived from objects actually observed or experienced. It usually involves a simplification and/or rearrangement of natural objects to meet the needs of artistic organization or expression. Sometimes there is so little resemblance to the original object that the shapes seem to have no relationship to anything ever experienced in our natural environment.

Nonobjective: An approach to art in which the visual signs are entirely imaginative and do not derive from anything ever seen by the artist. The shapes, their organization, and treatment by the artist are entirely personalized and consequently not associated by the observer with any previously experienced natural form.

Academic: A term applied to any kind of art which stresses the use of accepted rules for technique and form organization. It represents the exact opposite of the original approach which results in a vital, individual style of expression.

Subject matter: This term in a descriptive style of art refers to the persons or things represented as well as the artist's experiences which serve as his inspiration. In abstract or nonobjective forms of art it merely refers to the basic character of all the visual signs employed by the artist. In this case the subject matter has little to do with anything as experienced in the natural environment.

Form: The arbitrary organization or inventive arrangement of all of the visual elements according to principles which will develop an organic unity in the total work of art.

Content: The essential meaning, significance, or aesthetic value of an art form. It refers to the sensory, psychological, or emotional properties which one tends to "feel" in a work of art as opposed to the perception of mere descriptive aspects.

Realism: A form of expression which retains the basic impression of visual reality but, in addition, attempts to relate and interpret the universal meanings which lie underneath the surface appearance of natural form.

5

MEANING OF "ART"

Art has meant different things to different people at different times. The term as we use it today probably derives from the Renaissance words *arti* and *arte*. *Arti* was the designation for the craft guilds of the fourteenth, fifteenth and sixteenth centuries to which the artists were closely tied by the traditions of their calling. *Arte,* the word for craftsmanship, implied a knowledge of *materials* used by the artist, such as the chemical nature of his pigments and their interaction with one another, as well as the *grounds* on which a painter applied those pigments. *Arte* or craftsmanship also implied a skillful handling of those materials in the sense of producing images more or less like those of nature, but certainly not in the sense of imitating the exact appearance of nature. Art in the Renaissance thus served as both a technical and an interpretive record of human experience; it has continued to fulfill this function down to the present time although more meagerly at some times than others. In the nineteenth century, emphasis was often placed on the technical aspects of art, but, in the hands of the greatest masters, it always remained "interpretive."

Art deals with *visual signs* to convey ideas, moods, or generalized emotional experiences. It may be called a *language of visual signs.* Unlike the language of words, however, art is not meant to be informative. Information is the province of *symbols,* as in the words of literature, or the numbers of mathematics. Sometimes in the interpretation of ideas or moods, however, the artist may employ visual symbols, but the meaning of such symbols is embodied in the forms or images which the artist creates, just as are the ideas, moods, or experiences he conveys.

Since art is not intended to convey facts or information, the *appreciation* of art (by which we mean understanding art) may be enhanced when the observer attempts to grasp the *meaning* of works of art through intuition or instinct.

Although the observer may realize that the language of words and of visual signs as used in art are disparate, he may not recognize the varied problems of understanding and explaining art that arise. The limitations of the printed or spoken word in fully explaining art must be accepted as the natural inability of one medium to replace another. We have all felt the frustration which accompanies our attempts to describe a moving experience to a friend. We are soon convinced that the only description lies in the experience itself. Nonetheless, for education in the better understanding of art, the medium of words has to be used in order to attempt to explain the *nature* of art and the *ideas* presented by works of art.

Unfortunately the most moving experiences are usually those which are least expressible no matter how much we may wish to share them. The sensations of experience vary according to the senses which are stimulated, and, since certain major divisions of art developed around each of these senses, we may assume that certain qualities exist which make these means separate and unique.

MAJOR FORMS OF ART

The means which are most frequently used to convey human feelings are prose, poetry, music, the dance, the cinema, the theater, and the plastic and graphic arts. Subdivisions of the last two groups include painting, prints, drawing, sculpture, ceramics, and architecture. Each of these divisions exists to fulfill a specific need and therefore has its own province of expression. For example, one cannot paint a very successful picture of a novel, describe a melody, or dance a poem. There have always been attempts to extend the limits of art, but they have been successful only insofar as they have respected the particular properties of the medium of translation.

Opera, the theater, and the cinema are fields in which other arts are often introduced. They are rarely equally successful in all departments. Each medium contains its own problems, hence, with so many demands to be met, it is obvious that concessions must be made. As an analogy, the building of a house requires the sacrifice of some structural strength for lighting and visibility, living space for storage, utility for beauty, and so forth; each house represents a series of compromises according to the determinants of site, climate, the taste of the architect, owner, and builder, and finances available. The house which loses least in the inevitable series of compromises is, in the end, the most organically successful *design*. This is equally true of the composite art divisions.

There have been periods in which one or several of the *media* or art forms have enjoyed unusual interest. The people of the Italian Renaissance made art the measure of all things, and their lives were motivated by its enjoyment. Accomplishments in other fields were measured by their "artfulness," even to the extent that war itself became a work of art (Machiavelli).

Though each of the arts found its enthusiastic audience, the epicenter of the arts lay in painting and sculpture. Here, as elsewhere, the themes depicted were usually of religious origin, and of greatest interest to the people from the standpoint of *subject matter*. But the interest in the subject was equalled by the enthusiasm for the revolutionary concepts of *form* which derived from classical examples, and had been largely ignored during the intervening years. The transition from Medieval to Renaissance style, based on the Graeco-Roman style of antiquity, produced a remarkable *form-consciousness* in the populace, and introduced a period of history which was unique in its agree-

Figure 1. SPRING (PRIMAVERA) by Sandro Botticelli. This is an excellent example of an early Italian Renaissance work of art whose subject, while based on classical mythology, also infers a Christian theme. Venus, for example, was not only *classical* in concept, but symbolizes the Virgin Mary. The three part composition, which was of Roman origin, may be said to symbolize the Christian Trinity; the classically-derived dancing nymphs may be reinterpreted as representations of Christian angels.

Courtesy Alinari-Art Reference Bureau, Ussizi Gallery, Florence

ment on the value of art, and on its aesthetic. However, the advances which marked this revised outlook eventually became ends in themselves, leading to emphasis on scale and technical facility. In addition, art's alliance with the growth of scientific method at times produced a "scientific art" which was cold, calculated, and a product of conformity to standardized rules.

NARRATION AND DESCRIPTION IN ART

The layman continues to assume that art works should be recognizable or tell a story in a visually descriptive manner. It is true that some great works of art in the past have often told stories, but there is no inherited obligation on the part of artists to narrate, since it is not directly a part of their medium. Even when artists have chosen to narrate, their pictorial story may be visualized in many ways due to the nature of artistically expressed form.

In the nineteenth century, when the influence of poetry and prose reached its zenith, art often became a handmaiden of literature and, aided by science, attempted a factual interpretation of romantic and allegorical writing. There was a marked abandonment of *form* as an expressive agent in its own right while the favored subject matter was saturated with emotion and sentimentality. The role of art became *narrative* and *descriptive*, as though one attempted to give the feeling of battle by counting the troops and weapons, or tried to give the expression of mother love by taking an inventory of nursery

Figure 2. THE NUT GATHERERS by Adolphe William Bouguereau. An abandonment of *form* as a means of expression in which the *subject matter* is saturated with sentimentality and is essentially descriptive in nature.
Courtesy The Detroit Institute of Arts.

equipment. In short, artists had de-emphasized the essential ingredient of art and had made it become a second rate translator of other media.

Art must, in its way, narrate and describe to some degree, for it is a medium developed out of man's need for a particular type of communication. However, art is at its best when its *form* communicates directly, with *subject matter* and *symbols* playing subordinate roles. The mechanics of art reception are quite different from those of other media. An art work does not flow in time; it does not involve physical anticipation as in turning the pages of a book or listening for the next measure of music. The complete unity of a painting registers in a moment. The totality of the work can be taken in with one hard look, although this is hardly the recommended procedure for real appreciation. Hence, art does not lend itself wholeheartedly to the recitation of action in sequence form as does literature which is unfolding in its presentation. Narration is more properly a *by-product* of the artist's search.

ILLUSION AND REALITY IN ART

Similarly, art is, by its very nature, more a matter of illusion than the other forms of expression, music excepted. Action is never really present in paint or stone, and the actual human body plays no part in its expression as in the theater or dance. Although the artist activates his tools in the creation of a work of art, in the work itself such activity has become static and but a reminder of the past activity. Such a reminder of past activity may be stimulating in a manner somewhat like that of the present movement in the theater and the dance, but it is "illusive" and not "real." Because of this gulf between art and objective reality there seems little excuse for forcing art into a completely "realistic" or descriptive role. All media employ calculated deceits which help to create the "unrealistic" or imaginative atmosphere in which lies the unique value and appeal of the arts.

We certainly do not go to a play because we expect a duplication of everyday life. Instead we presumably hope to be transported into situations which, through the imagination and perception of the artist, exalt and come to grips with the fundamental forces of life. The make-believe deception in a theatrical production is purposely emphasized by our isolation from the stage, the unnatural postures and diction of the actors, exaggerated costumes, and countless other stratagems. Unreality is sought in varied ways in the other arts, always serving to draw man out of himself into a world of separate, yet meaningfully related existence. Yet, despite all this evidence of admittedly premeditated and justifiable guile, there are those who would miscast art in the role of a mirror of our practical everyday world. Imagination, invention, daring are ignored in favor of routine, rules and rote, and unremitting slavishness to visual details which even photography avoids through manipulations of focus and timing. Art which places chief emphasis on accuracy of description is essentially repetitive rather than creative.

"Reality," as it has been used here, is a term of convenience for the identification of the most common and superficial sensations of life. Even in this sense one could extend the description by pointing out that variations in physical and mental makeup among individuals create differences of sensation in those individuals, and thus, varying ideas of reality. Art, of course, constitutes an outlet for these differences of opinion. The genuine reality for each of us is defined by our most personal experiences and interests, producing a specialized outlook. As we progress in our studies in any field, we experience a change of mind as to the truly important factors in that area. As we dig more deeply into the fields of the intellect and the subconscious, we become aware that more basic realities underlie the appearances of commonplace experience.

It is this reality of broader and deeper understanding which marks the work of the true creator. Einstein shared the conventional patterns of life with the rest of us, but his perception revealed relationships which have helped to reshape our views of the world and our place in it. Between the world of convention and the world of perception there can be little doubt as to which, for Einstein, was the truer reality. Beethoven was very little different from the rest of us anatomically, but inwardly, he sensed revolutionary sounds which, in an abstract way, expressed the experiences and hopes of the human race. This, to Beethoven, was the true reality, not the payment of rent, the eating of meals, the reading of the evening newspaper. These two men and all those of equal significance contributed a fundamental theory of reality as discovered and transmitted through the medium in which they worked. Our society, receiving this creativity, gradually and often unconsciously experiences a parallel change in its own point of view. Creative men alter the frames of reference through which we see the things about us.

SPECIAL NATURE OF ARTISTIC EXPERIENCE

In reference to the foregoing, works of art may be called unique *form experiences* intended to invoke sensations in the observer. They are "unique" because they are different from objects and incidents of everyday association, even though the artist may have used such objects or incidents as subjects. One should see a work of art from the special frame of reference of aesthetic or artistic experience. When looking at a piece of sculpture, for example, we have a special attitude which is not present when seeing an ordinary chair. Both forms stand on all sides surrounded by space, but the chair is seen as having a special function. On the other hand, the sculptural form is intended to arouse subtle emotional states in the observer having nothing to do with use.

This very uniqueness of works of art sets them apart from functional or commonplace objects of everyday use; yet, most people fail to make a distinction in regard to art. When they want to know what a painting is "about," they have the same attitude towards the painting as towards any ordinary object of use. Of course, a chair, let us say, may not be of practical usefulness only but also a work of art. When this takes

place, added dimensions of *meaning* and *significance* are found along with the usual commonplace meaning of practical use.

With the distinction of this added uniqueness in mind, the observer should be able to approach works of visual art as he would poetry, as opposed to a scientific treatise, or as he would a symphony or jazz concert, as opposed to a commercial jingle on television.

Thus, we may call a painting or sculpture, the "objectification," "record," or "expression" of an artist's experiences during the age and place in which he lives. In this way it is opposed to the products of the industrial designer, or architect which also have the practical associations engendered by their forms. Again, a work of art may be defined as a kind of "autobiography" of an artist's attitudes in *line, value, shape, texture* and *color* which the uninitiated observer must learn to read.

The mind determines "how" and "what" we see and mental activity is necessary before the subtle qualities or characterful nuances of painting or sculpture are discernible. This is similar to the way in which hearing the handsome inflections of metric rhyme in poetry or melodic counterpart of music requires training by experience.

The province of the artist is to enlarge our comprehension of the world or universe, to widen our imaginative horizons, and to enrich our sensory enjoyment of all things. In order to do this, the artist is obliged to create new forms by the *selection, rearrangement,* or *exaggeration* (*distortion*) of those forms he sees or experiences about him in his environment. It is this environmental influence that causes the artist to reflect the time and place of his endeavours.

Twentieth-century artists may be credited with reasserting this creative principle which is fundamental to the visual arts. This principle was largely neglected during the nineteenth century when rapid scientific, industrial, and geographic expansion caused both artists and the public to think of art as a kind of science or mechanically learned skill. When the invention of the camera in the nineteenth century gradually obviated the representation of nature as a primary goal, artists began to reassert this principle.[1] They realized that there was no such thing as a "correct procedure" for originality, and that there was no basic "right" or "wrong" way to create. Artists began to see that the most *effective* art form was the most *unique* form; and, by its very uniqueness, it was most communicative of the ideas and feelings of the artist.

On the other hand, the public still tends to think of art in nineteenth-century terms. A surprisingly large number apparently believe that art should *imitate* nature, and that the best artists are those who make the most faithful duplication. A large part of the art of this century has little resemblance to nature forms; however, the backward-thinking layman seems to assume that the artist has either not achieved the skills necessary to duplicate nature, or that he is merely seeking notoriety by sensational images. Since art is not a science, or a technical performance in which the main aim is the surface description of objects, the sympathetic student must realize the nature and function of art before he can understand the goals he should try to achieve in studio performance.

The student must reorient himself away from a type of art that has as its highest aim the descriptive or factual rendition of subject matter. After practicing with the devices which may be found by analyzing works of art, the student may eventually find that these become instinctive tools of expression. Then, like most professional artists of today (who are concerned with what people feel and think about, their tragedies, hopes, joys and aspirations) the student may be able to conceive or imagine forms in an original way.

COMPONENTS OF A WORK OF ART

In order to approach art from the angle of expressing *meanings* and *ideas*, the student will first need to know something of the ingredients or components which make up a work of art. These ingredients are: The *Subject Matter*, the *Form*, and the *Content* or *Meaning* of a work.

Subject Matter

There is nearly always *subject matter* in a work of art. This is true even when the form-style is *abstract* (subject matter is limited insofar as it may be based on perceivable objects from nature). *Subject matter* in *abstract* art may lie more in the realm of 'ideas" or of intellectual concepts which are abstruse rather than based on material objects or facts. However, even in works of art which may be more obviously based on a representation of perceivable objects, the *subject matter* or object used is not of importance in itself to the artist. Subjects which the artist uses are merely a *stimulus to creativity*. It is the artist's initial response to *subject matter* and the way thereafter in which he presents the subject that is of importance. In addition, the artist during the course of progress in giving *form* to his subject may reinterpret its character; thus, the final form of the work of art may be far removed, in terms of what the observer sees, from the *original* subject, or even the original *response* of the artist to that subject.

The most significant problem in creating works of art is not "what" one uses as a subject, therefore, but "how" one interprets a subject in order to achieve character. The "how" of works of art involves the other ingredients of the art product—*Form* and *Content*. These are the most important components of a work of art.

Form

By *form* we mean the totality of the work of art. *Form* is the organization (design) of all elements which make up the work of art. Another way of defining this term is: the use made of the *visual devices* available to the artist. The visual devices or *elements* of *form*, as we tend to call them, are: *lines, shapes, values (varied lights* and *darks), textures,* and *colors.* The use to which the artist puts these elements determines the final appearance of his work of art.

Colorplate 1

Colorplate 2

---

[1]The term *representation* really means to *re-present*, as opposed to the direct presentation of meaning desirable in art forms.

principles of organization

The use of the *elements* concerns the particular physical and psychological relationships made between *visual devices* which in some way seem to affect us in their own right; that is, each element individually seems to have *intrinsic (inbuilt)* effects which are multiplied and made richer in their impact upon us when used in combinations.

The physical relationships of the elements are founded upon traditional, nearly universal *principles,* called generally the *principles of organization* or of *design,* or as in the past at times, *rules of composition* (i.e. *balance, rhythm, domination, harmony,* etc.). Some artists use these principles more consciously or logically than others, but all artists can be said to have at least an instinctive sensitivity to the value of *organization.* These *principles of organization* will be taken up in more detail later on in the text; they should be regarded as guides, not dogmatic rules, else the expressive quotient of *form* may be lost and the work may become *academic.* Nevertheless, throughout the history of art, it is in the area of basic principles by which works of art are given order that men have most often agreed lies the locus of "beauty" in art. Thus "beauty," an abstract concept, becomes tangible and universal in terms of *form organization* in art; hence terms like "beauty of form" or "formal beauty" are often applied to great works of art.

media and technique

Form-ordering is not only concerned with the *visual devices* and principles of relating said devices, but also with the *materials (media)* (i.e. pigments, inks, graphite) and the *tools* (i.e. brushes, pens, pencils) used by the artist, and with the manner *(technique)* in which these are used. *Technique* in painting, drawing and print-making also has to bring into artistic consideration the support, ground, or surface on which the artist applies his materials. While this is also true of the *spatial arts* of sculpture, architecture and three-dimensional design where materials are more directly a part of artistic execution, it does not seem to be such a separate consideration as with the two-dimensional arts.

organic unity—form organization

The real *feeling* of a work of art cannot be exposed by a breakdown of its parts. However, for the purposes of illustration and instruction we are often compelled to isolate the elements composing the *form* of the work. One could make a comparison with the parts of a radio and the parts or *elements of form* in a painting. If we should break down the radio and spread all the parts before us so that we were forced to examine each one separately, the form of the radio, as well as its meaning and function, would be lost to us. We could then put these parts together in such a way that a completely new device has been created. This contrivance would have the form of something not then recognizable (because it is outside human experience) nor even graced by a name. It would certainly not be the *form* of a radio, despite the presence of all the *parts* which are needed to make a radio. The device obviously would not fit our idea of *radio form* until all the parts were once again assigned their original positions. Once reassembled, the radio would work just as a competent art form "works," although the elusive property of life, in a work of art as in a human body, is impossible to define effectively. This difficulty stems from the fact that we can recognize life when all the parts are working, but we do not know what has been lost when they cease to work; life, like electricity, remains a mystery to us.

The anatomical parts of a painting which the artist manipulates are the *elements of form* which were previously listed. The artist hopes to assemble these in such a way that they will work together to create a meaningful *organic or "living" unity.* The result may be a hybrid work (similar to the device mentioned in the radio analogy) which functions only as a series of parts, and which consequently has no *unity of meaning and function.* On the other hand, he may be successful in creating a work in which each of the parts is vital, not by itself but in the general functioning of the work as a whole. In such an ideal development, the total organization or *form* cannot be conceived when any one of its parts is missing. With such a work, an entity is created which, like the radio, has a separate and distinct personality but, unlike the radio, is incapable of being named or classified, except according to a broad category. A radio would not ordinarily be confused with a chair, for each has its own characteristic distribution of *form* in which all those things have been eliminated that do not serve the particular utility of those objects. So it is with a distinguished work of art; every part aids in the purpose of expression. The paintings, as an entity, is inconceivable without those parts, and we can therefore say that it demonstrates perfect *unity* or total *form organization*. We could go farther and say that, although there are many identical radios of a particular model, there are qualities in every art work which tend to make it unlike any previously created; in the best sense of the word it is truly "original."

In the studio, the use of the suggestions offered in this book should place emphasis on the practice and observation of the potentialities for *form building* and on psychological or *expressive* impact.

Content or Meaning

When we begin to attempt to analyze *why* form affects us emotionally or expressively, or stimulates intellectual activity on the part of the observer, we are concerned with *Content* or *Form-Meaning*, the third component of a work of art. This component is the one in which the *quality* or *significance* of a work of art seems to reside. We may define *content* as the final statement, mood, or spectator experience with the work of art. It can also be called the *significance* of the *art form*; the kinds of emotions, intellectual activity, or associations we make between art objects, and our subconscious or conscious experiences seem to arise out of an *art form* and are completely inseparable from it except for purposes of discussion. In other words, *content* is the essential *meaning* of *form*. As Frank J. Mather points out in *Concerning Beauty*, "Meaning and Form are merely two aspects of the same thing—a form containing and conveying a meaning cast in a form in order that it may be expressed."[2]

Considering for a moment the present-day abstract approach to form on the part of many artists, wherein the form is decorative or patterned, there seems to be little if any *meaning*. However, there *is* meaning because there is no *form*, artistic or otherwise, which, in some way, does not have *meaning* for someone. In *abstract art*, it may be the unobvious but direct meaning inherent in a visual relationship, such as a black line set off against colored shapes of varied contours (see example by Wassily Kandinsky). Abstract artists obviously must find much that is pleasurable in such artistic arrangements, and the *form-conscious* observer may also feel this kind of *enjoyment-meaning* to be found in a well organized relationship of artistic elements.

abstraction

Sheldon Cheney says "Abstraction is an idea stripped of its concrete accompaniments, an *essence* or *summary*."[3] However, everyone abstracts the experiences that are of value to him from environment, and these are not necessarily concrete if they lie within the realm of the intuition or the imagination. In art, if one only takes away a few of the surface effects from what is usually considered "real" or tangible, he is abstracting in a limited way. The artist who draws a "tree" as closely as he can to the optical appearance of an actual tree is still abstracting his idea of "tree" in order to put it down in the graphic signs of art. In art terminology, however, we usually reserve the term *abstract art* for a type of form arrangement in which the *concept* of relating artistic devices (or *formal elements*) is more important than any indication of the perceivable objects which the artist may have seen in nature and used as *subject matter*.

Colorplate
3

[2]Mather, Frank J., *Concerning Beauty*, Princeton University Press, New Jersey, 1935, p. 128.
[3]Cheney, Sheldon, *Expressionism in Art*, Liveright Publishing Corp., 1934, p. 80.

nonobjective art

There are some artists who use *motifs* entirely from within themselves, rather than observing them in nature. Such artists begin with *form,* such as areas of color or of line and value, and arrive at artistic conclusions with these elements alone. Such artists have been called *nonobjective,* since they never resort to the use of natural objects believing them inconsequential in artistic expression. Artists of this persuasion "feel" natural objects are unimportant as subjects because they believe the work of art should "live" on its own merits.

Within these generally inclusive terms of *abstract* and *nonobjective* art, many diverse form concepts have developed over the years since 1910-1911. Perhaps the style in art called "Abstract-Expressionism" should be mentioned as an extension of *abstract* and *nonobjective* art. It seems that artists interested in this style have often abandoned the predilection for geometric planes found in *abstract* and *nonobjective* art in favor of emotional freedom and amorphous shapes.

Colorplate 4

form-meaning

Despite the fact that the terms *abstract* and *nonobjective* may tend to bring to mind that "nothing is perceivable in such works"; in view of the preceding explanation that concepts or ideas are manifest in such works (and these are equally valid as subject matter along with natural objects for the artist); it does not mean that such works have no content. *Content* or *meaning* lies in the *form* and is effective in so far as the observer is conversant with *form-meaning.*

There is little doubt, however, that the public has had its vision conditioned to "read" form representationally, in much the same sense that a snapshot represents nature in an "optical" manner. Of course, as suggested earlier, photography also may be handled less in this "optical" or mechanical manner and more in an artistic fashion. Such images will probably not appeal as much to the "object-minded" person but may have a certain acceptance for their technological value. Such individuals tend to look for similarly descriptive values in art and are only happy when *natural-appearing* objects are produced that provide an obvious basis of recognition.

With sufficient experience in looking at work of art, however, most individuals will eventually begin to realize that no particular emphasis on visual description of objects is needed; for them painting and sculpture may be optically understandable and yet have character above and beyond ordinary description. Almost anyone can sense the universal quality of serenity in a Cézanne landscape (*The Stockade*); or the impassioned response to objects and life expressed by Van Gogh (as in his *Cypress Landscape*). Van Gogh has depicted the quality of nature as a living, stimulating force in such a way as to make his painting become a vital expression in its own right. This is made possible through the swirling shapes, the direct clash of colors, and the heavily pigmented surface. The meaning of "city" in the illustration by Stuart Davis should be apparent in his machine-like shapes, and movement-tensions, all of which are a part of his *form concept.*

aesthetic experience

Previously in this chapter it was mentioned that the quality or significance of a work of art lies in our interpretation of the *content.* We called this the *aesthetic* value of the work of art. The experiencing of a work of art, when it is enjoyable, persuasive, stimulating, disturbing, or otherwise evocative of our senses, is an *aesthetic* or artistic experience. This is meaningful and of value to us because it is *really* what we hope to experience when we look at works of art. Obvious recognition of common, everyday items carried over into art cannot make this much of an artistic experience, hence, not *meaningful* in the deepest sense as art. It merely has some small item of value on an associational basis, but once we have identified the object, we are done with the form and forget it. Works of art are *meaningful* when they seem to remain a *part of us* after we have left them. If we are inclined to come back and see them again, we have had a worthwhile experience

Colorplate 1. BEDROOM AT ARLES by Vincent van Gogh. The subjects or objects used are not of importance in themselves to artists, as in the case of still-life objects which are often used by artists as subjects. The subject is merely a *stimulus* to creativity, but what makes this van Gogh of value and unique from other paintings, his own or those by other artists, is the presentation.

Courtesy The Art Institute of Chicago.

Colorplate 2. WINTER (RETURN OF THE HUNTERS) by Pieter Brueghel, Kunsthistorisches Museum, Vienna. The visual devices of line direction, spotting of light and dark areas, of rhythmic repetition of similar shape patterns, and the sense of spatial indication all contribute to the total pictorial organization which is called FORM.

Courtesy Art Reference Bureau.

Colorplate 3. COMPOSITION #3 by Wassily Kandinsky. In *abstract* art there *is* CONTENT, but it may be the unobvious form meaning inherent in a visual relationship, such as a black line, or lines set-off against colored shapes of varied contours.

Collection The Museum of Modern Art, New York. Mrs. Simon Guggenheim Fund.

Colorplate 4. THE STARRY NIGHT by Vincent van Gogh. Van Gogh's impassioned response to life can be seen in his swirling shapes, intensity of colors and heavily pigmented surfaces.

Courtesy The Museum of Modern Art, New York. Lillie P. Bliss Bequest.

Figure 3. HOUSE BY THE RAILROAD by Edward Hopper. The passive serenity of this painting has a character above and beyond ordinary description.

Courtesy The Museum of Modern Art, New York.

that does not terminate at the instant we have "seen" but one aspect. It is not enough, therefore, that art forms be merely associated with natural objects or natural forms. A "good" work of art must be "seen" by the observer as well as the artist with *aptness*, power of expression, and flexibility.

When art represents natural objects, many people continue to assume that it is meant to tell a visual story; but let us remember from our earlier discussion of this point that narration is really the province of literature. What the observer must learn to look for in works of art

are not specifically recognizable associations with objects, stories, or events in life, but a general *expression* of general experiences provided by the artist in new forms—and thus, with uncommon *meaning* or aesthetic significance.

It is, perhaps, interesting to note at this point, that the *naturalist* style of the 1870's and 1880's in France, which has tended to be maintained as the layman's "norm of vision" down to mid-twentieth century, was at its time a *new form* of art based on the science-centering of culture resulting from the Industrial Revolution. As a new *form of art* with unfamiliar meanings for its

Figure 4. NEW YORK WATERFRONT by Stuart Davis. The meaning of "city" to Stuart Davis should be apparent to the observer in his machine-like shapes, brilliant color, and moving tensions.

Courtesy The Museum of Modern Art, New York.

time, *naturalism* was largely rejected or neglected by the public in about the same manner as most people of our time react to the art of today.

Having now studied the main points of theory dealing with the *nature of art,* the student should move on to a study of the chapters on the *form elements* and their possibilities, and then attempt to put into practice the suggestions offered. It should be understood that outside a further theoretical discussion, as in this chapter, the studio teacher cannot really "teach" the *Subject Matter, Form,* or *Content* of works of art, but can only expose the student to *experiences* in the area of these components.

CHAPTER 3: FORM

Definitions:

Balance: A feeling of equality in weight, attention, or attraction of the various visual elements within the pictorial field as a means of accomplishing organic unity.

Symmetrical balance: A form of balance achieved by the use of identical compositional units on either side of a vertical axis within the confining pictorial space.

Asymetrical balance: A form of balance attained when the visual units on either side of a vertical axis are not identical but are placed in positions within the pictorial field so as to create a "felt" equilibrium of the total form concept.

Approximate symmetry: The use of forms which are similar on either side of a vertical axis. They may give a feeling of the exactness of equal relationship but are sufficiently varied to prevent visual monotony.

Elements of art structure: The basic visual signs as they are combined into optical units which are used by the artist to communicate or express his creative ideas. The combination of the basic elements of line, shape, value, texture, and color represent the visual language of the artist.

Dominance: The principle of visual organization which suggests that certain elements should assume more importance than others in the same composition. It contributes to organic unity by emphasizing the fact that there is one main feature and that other elements are subordinate to it.

Harmony: The unity of all of the visual elements of a composition achieved by the repetition of the same characteristics or those which are similar in nature.

Motif: A visual element or a combination of elements which is repeated often enough in a com-position to make it the dominating feature of the artist's expression.

Pattern: The obvious emphasis on certain visual form relationships and certain directional movements within the visual field. It also refers to the repetition of elements or the combinations of elements in a readily recognized systematic organization.

Picture Plane: The actual flat surface on which the artist executes his pictorial image. In some cases it acts merely as a transparent plane of reference to establish the illusion of forms existing in a three-dimensional space.

Picture Frame: The outermost limits or boundary of the picture plane.

Positive Shapes: The enclosed areas which represent the initial selection of shapes planned by the artist. They may suggest recognizable objects or merely be planned non-representational shapes.

Negative areas: The unoccupied or empty space left after the positive shapes have been laid down by the artist; however, because these areas have boundaries, they also function as shapes in the total pictorial structure.

Repetition: The use of the same visual element a number of times in the same composition. It may accomplish a dominance of one visual idea, a feeling of harmonious relationship, or an obviously planned pattern.

Rhythm: A continuance, a flow, or a feeling of movement achieved by the repetition of regulated visual units.

Unity: The whole or total effect of a work of art which results from the combination of all of its component parts.

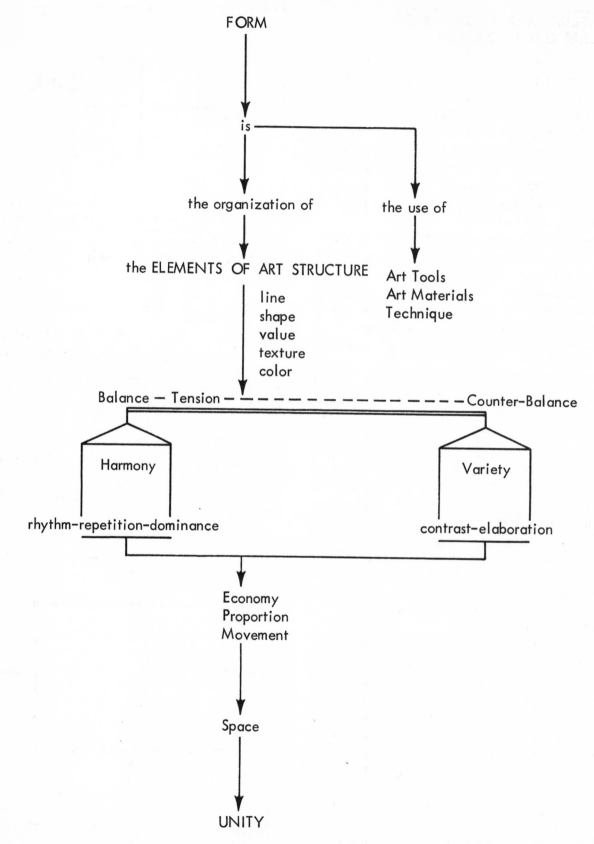

Figure 5.

PRELIMINARY FACTORS OF FORM ORGANIZATION

In a completed work of art, there are three components, common denominators which change only in emphasis. These components are so interwoven that to isolate any one of them would mean total disorder. The whole work of art is always more important than any one of its components. In this chapter emphasis is placed on the component, *form*, in order to theorize and investigate some of the physical principles of visual order.

In seeing images, one takes part in *visual forming* (or ordering). In this act, the eye and mind organize visual differences by integrating optical units into a unified whole. The mind instinctively tries to create order out of chaos. This order adds an equilibrium to human visual experience which would otherwise be confusing and garbled.

The artist is a visual former with a plan. With his materials, he arranges the *elements for his form-structure*: *lines, shapes, values, textures* and *colors*. The elements he uses need to be controlled, organized, and integrated. This the artist manages through the binding qualities of the *principles of organization*: *balance, harmony, variety, movement, proportion* and *space*. The sum total of these, assuming the success of his plan and its execution, equal *unity*. Unity in this instance means *oneness*, an organization of parts which fit into the order of a whole and become vital to it.

Picture Plane

There are many ways to begin a work of art. However, it is generally accepted that the picturemaker must begin with a flat surface. To the artist, the flat surface is the *picture plane* on which he executes his pictorial image. The flat surface further represents an imaginary plane through which his picture is seen. This plane establishes by comparative relationships all other lines, planes, directions, and movements in the space on, behind, and in front of it. In this instance, the picture plane is used as a basis for judging two- and three-dimensional space.

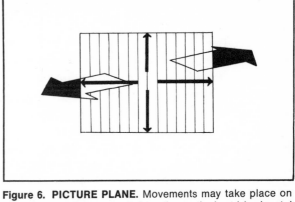

Figure 6. PICTURE PLANE. Movements may take place on the flat surface as indicated by the vertical and horizontal arrows. The vertical lines represent an imaginary plane through which a picture is seen. The artist may also give the illusion of advancing and receding movement in space as shown by the two large arrows.

Picture Frame

A picture is limited entirely to the *picture frame* which, by definition, is described as the outermost limits or the boundary of the *picture plane*. The picture frame should be clearly established at the beginning of a pictorial organization; once its shape and proportion are defined, all of the art elements and their employment will be influenced by it. The first problem for the pictorial artist is to organize the elements of art within the picture frame on the picture plane.

Colorplates 5, 6

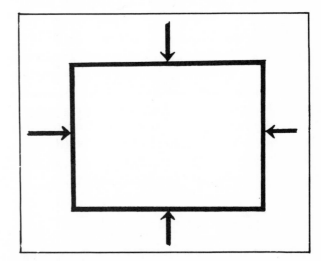

Figure 7. PICTURE FRAME. The picture frame represents the outermost limits or the boundary of the picture plane. These limits may be represented by the edges of the canvas or paper in which the artist works or the margin drawn within these edges.

The proportions and shapes of picture frames used by artists are varied. Squares, triangles, circles, and ovals have been used as frame shapes by the artist of the past, but the most popular is the rectangular frame which in its varying proportions offers the artist an interesting two-dimensional space variety. Many artists select the outside proportions of their pictures on the basis of geometric, mathematical formulas. These rules suggest dividing surface areas into odd proportions of 2 to 3 or 3 to 5 rather than equal relationships. The results are pleasing visual and mathematical spatial arrangements. After the picture frame has been established, the *elements of art*, their directions and movements, should be in harmonious relation to this shape; otherwise they will interrupt a main stream of *pictorial unity*.

Positive-Negative

Colorplate 7

All of the surface areas in a picture should contribute to total unity. Those areas which represent the initial selection of the artist in terms of recognizable objects or non-representational shapes are generally called *positive areas*. Unoccupied spaces are termed *negative areas*. These negative areas are just as important to total picture unity as are the positive units which are tangible and more explicitly laid down. Further, negative areas might be considered that portion of the picture plane which continues to show through after the positive units have been placed in a framed area. Traditionally, foreground positions were considered positive and background spaces negative.

The term *positive-negative* is important to the student who is investigating art organization since the beginner usually directs his attention to positive object units and neglects the surrounding spaces. The resulting pictures are generally overcrowded, busy, and confusing.

PRINCIPLES OF ORGANIZATION

The reader should be reminded, once again, that the *principles of organization* are only guides for seeing for the beginning student. They are *not* laws with only one interpretation

Figure 8.
Courtesy National Gallery of Art, Washington, D.C. Andrew Mellon Collection.

Figure 9.

POPE INNOCENT X by Diego Velazquez. The subject in this painting represents a *positive* shape which has been enhanced by careful consideration of the *negative* areas or the surrounding space. The dark area in Figure 9 indicates the *negative* shape and the white area the *positive* shape.

or application. The principles of organization may help in finding certain pictorial solutions for *unity*, but they are not ends in themselves and following them will not always guarantee the best results. Art works are created by personal interpretation and should be judged as total visual expressions.

Unity-Harmony and Variety

The artist can now set about organizing the elements of art in his plan. First, he must know what the controlling factors are in organizing.

Organization in art consists of developing a *unified* whole out of diverse units. This is done by relating contrasts through certain *transitional* means. To explain further, an artist might use in his pictures two opposing kinds of lines, vertical and horizontal. The *transitional passage* which could reconcile the difference between these two line-directions would be a straight-line type. Since both the horizontal and vertical lines are already straight this likeness of *type* would relate them. It would seem here that harmonious means are necessary to hold contrasts together. Unity and organization in art are dependent upon dualism; a balance between harmony and variety. This balance does not have to be of equal proportions; harmony might outweigh variety; or variety might outweigh harmony. Harmony is achieved on a picture surface through transitional rhythms and repetitions; variety through diversity and change. The problem for the artist is one of *balance* between harmony and variety.

Balance

Balance is so fundamental to unity that it is impossible to present the problems of organization without its consideration. At the simplest level, balance suggests a gravitational equilibrium of a single unit in space, or of pairs symmetrically arranged with respect to a central axis or point. Perhaps the balancing of pairs can be best illustrated by a weighing scale. Visually, this scale is associated with an apparatus for weighing which has a beam poised on a central pivot (the fulcrum) so as to move freely, with a pan on each end. In using such a scale, bal-

ance is achieved not through an actual physical weighing process, but through a visual judgment on the part of the observer based upon his past experiences and his knowledge of certain principles of physics. In this type of scale, the forces are balanced left and right or *horizontally* with respect to the supporting crossline. In the illustration of the horizontal balance scale, a line of one physical dimension balances or counterbalances a line with the same (or equal) physical characteristics. Other examples point out the balance between lines, shapes, and values which have been modified and varied. In the second type of weighing scale, forces are balanced *vertically*. The third illustrated weighing device points out not only a horizontal and vertical balance, but a balance of forces which are distributed around a center point. This is called a *radial* weighing scale.

Colorplate 8

In picture-making, balance refers to a "felt" optical equilibrium between all parts of the work. The artist balances forces horizontally, vertically, radially, diagonally in all directions and positions.

There are several *factors* which, when combined with the elements, contribute to balance in a work of art. These factors or variables are *position* or placement, *size, proportion, quality* and *direction* of the elements. Of these factors, *position* plays the lead role. If two shapes of equal physical qualities are placed near the bottom of a picture frame, the work will appear bottom-heavy or out of balance with the large upper space. Such shapes should be placed in positions which will contribute to the *total balance* of all the involved picture parts. Similarly, the other factors can put a pictorial arrangement "in" or "out" of balance according to their use.

In seeking balance, it should be recognized that the elements of art represent "moments of force." The eye, as it travels over the picture surface, pauses momentarily for significant picture parts which are contrasting in character. These contrasts represent moving and directional forces which must counterbalance one another so that a *controlled tension* results. In the painting, *Handball*, by Ben Shahn, "the moments of force" are felt in a tension which

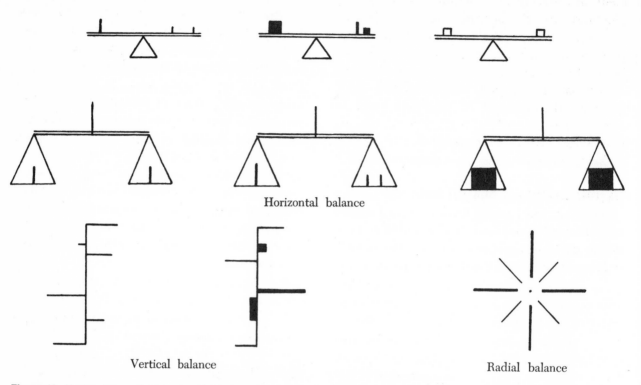

Horizontal balance

Vertical balance

Radial balance

Figure 10. Horizontal, vertical, and radial balance.

exists between the two figures in the foreground and the number 1 which has been placed on the top of the wall. These forces together support one another. The problem of visual balance has resulted in two basic types of organization, symmetrical and asymmetrical.

symmetrical (bisymmetrical or formal) balance

The beginner will find that *symmetry* is the simplest and most obvious type of balance. In "pure symmetry," identical *optical units* (or forces) are *equally* distributed on either side of a vertical axis or axes in mirror-like repetition. Because of its identical repetition, the effect of pure symmetrical balance is usually static, lifeless. It is simply too monotonous for prolonged audience-attention. However, through its use, *unity* is easily attained.

Approximate symmetry. The severe monotony of "pure symmetry" in pictorial arrangements is often relieved by a method which is some-

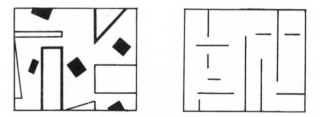

Figure 11. Balance in all directions, horizontal, vertical, radial, and diagonal.

times called "approximate symmetry." Here, the two sides of a picture are varied to hold audience-attention, but they are similar enough to make repetitious relationships and their vertical axis optically felt.

Radial balance. This is another type of pictorial arrangement which, through repetitive association, belongs to the family of symmetry. In radial balance two or more forces, which are identical in strength and character, are distributed around a center point. The balance of rotating forces creates a visual circular movement on the picture surface thus adding a new dimension to an otherwise static, symmetrical balance. Although "pure radial" balance opposes identical forces, interesting varieties can be created by means of spatial, numerical, and directional modification. In spite of such modifications, the principle of repetition must be stressed and the results create a decorative allover effect. Radial balance is chiefly used to make commercial decorative patterns.

asymmetrical (or occult) balance

Asymmetrical balance means a visual control of contrasts through a "felt" equilibrium between parts of a picture. For example, a "felt" balance might be achieved between a small area of strong color and a large empty space. Particular parts may be contrasting provided that they contribute to the allover balance of the total picture. There are no rules for achieving asymmetrical balance; there is no center point and no dividing axis. If, however, the artist can feel, judge or estimate the opposing forces and their tensions so that they balance each other in total concept, a vital, dynamic and expressive organization will result on the picture plane. A picture balanced by contradictory forces, for instance, black and white, blue and orange, shape and space, impels the further investigation of these relationships and thus becomes an inquiring and interesting visual experience.

Colorplate
9

Figure 12. HANDBALL by Ben Shahn.
Courtesy The Museum of Modern Art, New York. Donated by Mrs. John D. Rockefeller, Jr. Fund.

Figure 13. LAKE GEORGE WINDOW by Georgia O'Keeffe. The window, its moldings, and shutters are equally distributed on either side of an imaginary vertical axis in mirror-like repetition. Georgia O'Keeffe has balanced this painting symmetrically.

Courtesy The Museum of Modern Art, New York.

Figure 14. AMERICAN GOTHIC by Grant Wood. The two figures in this picture create repetitious relationships so that their *vertical axis* is optically felt. This may be termed *approximate symmetry.*

Courtesy The Art Institute of Chicago.

Harmony-Rhythm, Repetition, and Dominance

Colorplate
10

Rhythm, repetition, and *dominance* act as transitional agents for creating order out of forces which are otherwise in opposition. They relate picture parts. After a reconciliation has been effected between the forces in opposition, *harmony* will result on a picture surface. Harmony is a necessary ingredient to *unity*; likewise rhythm, repetition, and dominance are essential to harmony.

rhythm

Rhythm is the continuance; a flow, which is affected by reiterating and measuring related, similar or equal parts. It is recurrence, a measure, such as meter, tempo or beat. Walking, running, dancing, wood-chopping, hammering are human activities with recurring measures in them.

In art, if particular parts are recalled in a rhythmical way a work will be seen together. *Rhythm,* in this instance, has the effect of giving both *unity* and *balance* to a work of art.

Rhythm exists in many different ways on a picture surface. It may be *simple,* as when it repeats only one type measure; it may be *composite* of two or more recurring measures which exist simultaneously, or it may be a complex variation which recalls a particular accent in a usual way. José Clemente Orozco charges his pictures with an obvious rhythmical order. He used several rhythmical measures simultaneously to create a geometric unity. He welds his pictures together by repeating shape directions and edges, value differences, and color modifications.

Motif. In music, rhythm may be associated with theme which is repeated with simple variation throughout a score. The *motif* of a work of art is, perhaps, the equivalent of the *theme* in

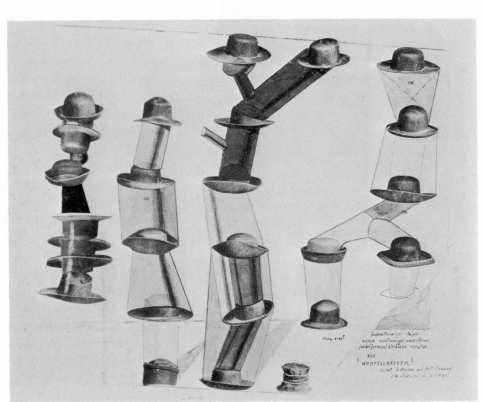

Figure 15. THE HAT MAKES THE MAN by Max Ernst. Motif: the hats in this picture represent strong *accents, motifs,* in a system of accents and pauses. Notice the variety of style, size, and shape contour within the repetitive order.

Courtesy The Museum of Modern Art, New York.

music. It might be described as a composite of several rhythmical measures, or it may be looked on as a picture within a picture. A motif may be *objective* as it borrows from nature; or it may be *invented*, drawing its inspiration from configurations found in the art elements, their direction or space.

Rhythm is not a single part; it is an order in the whole work. A motif in a picture, for example, is only one accent in a *system* of accents and pauses. Once the "beat" of this system is "felt" in an art work a visual organization will be formed.

Pattern. A pattern in a work of art is used to establish a harmonious relationship of parts, usually similar or repetitive in character. It will lead the eye in a movement from one element to another or from one accent to another. The handling and placement of a line, shape, value, texture or color will guide the underlying pictorial structure which is called pattern.

Rhythms, repetitions and their alternating pauses are systems which aid in the creation of pattern. The elements of art are interwoven with rhythmical repetitions, "beats," which pul-

Figure 16. PATTERNS. The lines in this student exercise are interwoven with rhythmical, repetitious "beats," which pulsate in flowing movement over the picture surface.

sate in movement from one picture part to another to create an order, a unity. Pattern is generally two-dimensional or *decorative* in character, and it emphasizes the unifying qualities of form.

repetition

Repetition and rhythm are inseparable. Rhythm is the *result* of repetition. Repetition is a method used to reemphasize visual units again and again in a marked pattern. It is an easy way to bind the work together, to achieve unity. By its insistence, repetition demands attention or emphasis, and it allows pause for examination.

Repetition does not always mean exact *duplication*, but it does mean similarity or *near-likeness*. Slight variations of a simple repetition will add absorbing interest to pattern which might otherwise be tiring.

Colorplate 11

dominance

Each particular part of a picture should receive its proper degree of *dominance* or emphasis. In order to merit attention, a featured part should be in contrast with its surrounding area. This dominating part becomes a point of interest which when distributed in a measured, repetitive order will create a high accent in a metered rhythm.

To conserve the energies of the viewer, a work of art should be rhythmically articulated. Without a rhythmic order of any kind, a picture surface would be fatiguing and chaotic. With a good rhythmical distribution of dominant picture parts, in a good working measure (meter), the duration of the viewer's attention will be enhanced.

Colorplate 12

Variety-Contrast and Elaboration

Harmony is the counter-weight of variety. It is the other side of organization which is essential to unity. With *harmony*, the artist binds the picture parts together into one whole; with *variety*, he adds interest to this total form. Here, interest refers to the ability of a work of art to hold the attention of a viewer. If the creator

combines visual forces which are all equal on a picture surface, he will find balance, but it will be static, lifeless and without tension. By adding variation to his picture forces, the artist attaches essential ingredients (i.e. diversion or change) for enduring attention.

The artist controls and uses variety in two ways. *First*, he finds variety in opposition or contrast, and he reconciles the visual differences to create unity. *Second*, the artist will *elaborate* upon forces which are equal in quality and strength; he does not work spontaneously, but he "reworks" picture areas persistently until a satisfactory solution is reached. The picture grows as the artist works. Surfaces become rich with interesting and subtle material changes; the theme develops dramatic strength; and the ensuing form attaches purposeful meaning.

Variations add vibrations to static picture surfaces. As in music, the contrasting forces act as modulators in changing the pitch or the vibrating qualities of a pictorial pattern. If the contrast is increased, the pitch is raised; as the differences are brought into close accord, the pitch is lowered. The pitch that sets the contrasts in order adds a dynamic vitality to pictorial organization.

Economy

Often, in the beginning of a creation, the parts become complicated, too important, and confusing. The result is disorganization or visual turmoil. Generally, these parts can be brought into agreement by *economically* sacrificing certain particulars and relating each part to the whole picture. Economy of expression is vital to unity. A picture should be composed in a simple, direct manner. There are no rules for using economy; if a part "works" in an organization with respect to the whole, it should be kept; if it disrupts the unity it should be "reworked" and reevaluated in a purposeful manner. Economy is often associated with the term *abstraction*, which, by its very definition, includes simplicity of means. The modern artist often sacrifices, abstracts so to speak, particular details in order to strengthen the organizing conclusions of his pictures.

Movement

A picture surface is static; its parts, in actuality, do not move. *Movement* in a work of art is implied so as to create life and activity in organization. The aim of movement, as it is used in connection with form, is to tie a picture together. It is the indication of eye travel through visual paths on the picture surface.

The elements of art structure and the many principles of organization contribute forces to movement. The direction and boundary of a shape may lead the eye from one position to another while a rhythmic repetition will guide its travel through associational means. Movement between colors and textures can be created

Figure 17.

Courtesy National Gallery of Art, Washington, D.C. Widener Collection.

Figure 18.

VENUS AND ADONIS by Titian. The movement in this painting was planned by Titian to carry the spectator's eye along guided visual paths. These were created (as is indicated by the accented lines in the diagram) by emphasizing the figure contours and the light values. The triangular shape made by the main figures serves as a pivotal motif around which secondary movements circulate.

by relating their values to one another. The purpose of movement, here, is to create unity with eye travel.

Proportion

Since *proportion* deals with the ratio of one part to another it must fall under the heading, "principles of organization." Ratio implies comparison; it is expressed in *size, number, position,* and *space*. In a picture, the relation of one size to another is always important. The artist tends to use sizes which seem to balance, are similar, and seem related by comparison. If he uses a large shape beside a small one, it will seem uncomfortable and out of scale. A shape should fit properly in its position and space; if it "feels" comfortable, it should be kept. "Fitting" requires a personal judgment on the part of the creator since there are no rules for presenting the "right" size, or the "correct" proportion. Here, once again, the artist must rely on harmony and variety for judging and evaluating the parts of his organization.

Space

The problems of *space* in art organization are of such great magnitude that an entire chapter is devoted to them later. It will suffice to mention here that space when used in a work of art should be *consistent*. There is nothing, by way of comparison, that can throw a picture so "out of kilter" as a jumbled spatial representation. If an artist begins his picture with one kind of spatial representation, he should continue to use the same qualities in the succeeding stages of his work. It is almost a necessity for an artist to preplan his space. This early planning will contribute immeasurably to the unity in any work of art.

Unity in art results from practicing, knowing, and selecting the "right" visual devices and using the best principles to relate them. An understanding of the principles of form structure is fundamental to art education. The investigations discussed in the previous chapters are only intellectual beginnings for seeing some of the vast possibilities in the creative art realm. By studying the principles of form organization, the beginner will gain an understanding that later will help him find *intuitive* and *creative* experiences.

The group of art elements; *lines, shapes, textures, values,* and *colors* cannot exist exclusively in themselves. There is often a constant overlapping of these art elements as they borrow from one another to become visible or more expressive.

Due to the fact that the art elements each have an intrinsic appeal, they will be separated in the following chapters for the purposes of individual study. When using two, three, or all of the elements in one picture, the elements can be separated only for the purpose of discussion. In reality, the artist must consider these elements together as contributing factors to one complete statement, the whole art work.

CHAPTER 4: LINE

Definitions:

Line: A line is the path of a moving point, that is, a mark made by a tool or instrument as it is drawn across a surface. It is usually made visible by the fact that it contrasts in value with the surface on which it is drawn.

Contour: A line which creates a boundary separating an area of space from its surrounding background.

Mass: A three-dimensional form or body which stands out from the space surrounding it because of difference in color, value, or texture.

Calligraphy: The use of flowing rhythmical lines which intrigue the eye as they enrich surfaces. Calligraphy is highly personal in nature similar to the individual qualities found in handwriting.

Plastic: A quality which emphasizes the three-dimensional nature of shape or mass. On a two-dimensional surface, plasticity is always an illusion created by the use of the visual elements in special ways.

Decorative: The quality which emphasizes the two-dimensional nature of any of the visual elements. Decoration enriches a surface without denying the essential flatness of its nature.

LINE IS THE ELEMENTARY MEANS OF VISUAL COMMUNICATION

Line is a graphic device made to function symbolically in artistic and literary expression. Its expression may be employed on *subjective* or *objective* levels. Objectively it may describe simple measurements and surface characteris-

tics. Subjectively it may be modified to suggest many emotional states and responses. Linear designs in the form of ideograms and alphabetical letters are used by man as a basic means of communication. The artist similarly uses line but in a more broadly communicative manner. Line seems to be fundamental in such expression; and, since the *elements of art structure* are to be studied separately, it seems appropriate to begin with *line*.

Line, as such, does not exist in nature; it is a man made invention, an *abstraction*, developed as an agent for the *simplification* of statements of visual fact and for *symbolizing* graphic ideas. Nature contains only *mass*, the measurements of which are conveniently demonstrated in art by the use of line as *contour*.

Line operates on elastic terms in the visual field. It may be an *edge*, as on a piece of sculpture; a *meeting of areas* where textural or color differences do not blend; a *contour* as it defines a drawn shape; *plastic* in so far as it suggests space; or *calligraphic* as it enriches a surface. The line may perform several of these functions at the same time. Its wide applications range into the creation of *value* and *texture* illustrating the impossibility of making a completely arbitrary and final distinction between the elements of art structure. However, it is possible to recognize and analyze the linear components of a work of art.

PHYSICAL CHARACTERISTICS OF LINES

The *physical* properties of line are: *measure, type, direction, location,* and *character.*

Measure

Measure refers to the length and width of line. A line may be of any length or shortness

Figure 19. *Objectively,* the line used here merely serves to describe *simple characteristics* of a female figure; however, from the *subjective* standpoint, the line has individual variations which represent the *feeling* of the individual artist toward the subject portrayed.

and breadth or narrowness. There are, therefore, an infinite number of combinations of long and short or thick and thin lines which, according to their use, may divide or unify the *pictorial area.*

Type

Any line is by its own nature a particular type. If the line continues in only *one* direction, it will be straight; if *gradual changes* of direction occur, it will be curved; if those changes are sudden and abrupt, an *angular* line will be created. In adding this dimension to that of *measure,* we find that long or short, thick or thin lines can be straight, angular or curved. The straight line in its continuity ultimately becomes *repetitious* and, depending on its length, either rigid or brittle. The curved line may curve to form an arc, reverse its curve to become wavy, or continue turning within itself to produce a spiral. The alterations of movement become *vis-*

Figure 20. THREE MUSICIANS by Fernand Léger. Léger uses line in an *abstract* manner to *simplify* complex forms, which exist in nature as *masses.*

Courtesy The Museum of Modern Art, New York. Mrs. Simon Guggenheim Fund.

Colorplate 5. THE VIRGIN WITH SAINT INÉS AND SAINT TECLA by El Greco. The rectangular frame shape, by its proportions, offers to the artist a pleasing and interesting spatial arrangement. Here, El Greco has elongated his main shapes to repeat and harmonize with the vertical character of the picture frame.

Courtesy The National Gallery of Art, Washington, D.C. Widener Collection.

Colorplate 6. THE ADORATION OF THE MAGI by Fra Angelico and Fra Filippo Lippi. The artists have used figures and architecture, the elements of art, their directions and movements in harmonious relation to a circular picture frame.

Courtesy The National Gallery of Art, Washington, D.C. Samuel H. Kress Collection.

Colorplate 7. A GIRL WITH A WATERING CAN by Auguste Renoir. Since the figure is located in the *foreground* of Renoir's painting, it is considered a *positive* unit. Traditionally, the surrounding *background* areas are considered negative space.

Courtesy The National Gallery of Art, Washington, D.C. Chester Dale Collection.

Colorplate 8. FISH MAGIC by Paul Klee. In this painting by Paul Klee, the object shapes through their repetition and transitional variation create harmonious relationships. Variety in *size* and *treatment* create contrasting notes which are balanced by the repetition of color and shape character

Courtesy Philadelphia Museum of Art. The Arensberg Collection.

Colorplate 9. FAMILY OF SALTIMBANQUES by Picasso. *Asymmetrical balance:* a "felt" balance is achieved through a juxtaposition of the varying shapes and a continuing distribution of similar values and colors.

Courtesy The National Gallery of Art, Washington, D.C. Chester Dale Collection.

Colorplate 10. ZAPATISTAS by José Orozco. *Rhythm:* A continuous *movement* is suggested as the Zapatistas cross the picture surface from right to left. In passing, these figures form a *repetitious beat;* as their shapes, leaning in the same direction, create a *rhythmic order.*

Courtesy The Museum of Modern Art, New York.

Colorplate 11. THE LOVERS by Pablo Picasso.
Economy: Pablo Picasso has simplified the complex qualities of the surface structures of his two figures. He has reduced the representation of his lovers to contour lines and flat color renderings. Here, Picasso has abstracted (used economical means) the two lovers in order to strengthen the expressive bond between them.

Courtesy The National Gallery of Art, Washington, D.C. Chester Dale Collection.

Colorplate 12. CHESTNUT TREES AT JAS DE BOUFFAN by Paul Cézanne. *Dominance:* the combined rhythms and repetitions of the chestnut trees in Cézanne's painting dominate his landscape.

Courtesy The Minneapolis Institute of Arts.

THE DREAM by Henri Rousseau. Rousseau, has used groupings of lines in a *decorative* manner to stimulate the feeling of the textural *pattern* in jungle growth.

Courtesy The Museum of Modern Art, New York. Gift of Nelson A. Rockefeller.

Colorplate 14. TRIO by Steve Magada. Line may be admired for its own sake. Steve Magada has exploited this appeal by creating a picture in which the linear effects are dominant.

Courtesy Steve Magada.

Colorplate 15. MONTJOIE SAINT DENIS! by Georges Mathieu. The use of red, yellow, dark blue (primary colors) and white in these lines serves to produce a forceful, strong, emotional effect.

Courtesy The Museum of Modern Art, New York. Gift of Mr. and Mrs. Harold Kaye.

ually entertaining and physically stimulating if *rhythmical.* A curved line is inherently graceful and, to a degree, unstable. The abrupt changes of direction in an angular line create excitement and/or confusion. Our eyes frequently find difficulty in adapting themselves to its unexpected deviations of direction. Hence, the angular line is one which is full of challenging interest.

Direction

A further complication of line is its *basic direction,* one which may exist irrespective of the component movements *within* the line. That is, a line may be a *zigzag type* but take a generally *curved direction.* Thus the *line type* may be contradicted or flattered by its *basic movement.* A generally horizontal direction could indicate serenity and perfect stability whereas a diagonal direction would probably imply agitation and motion. A vertical line generally speaks of such things as poise and aspiration. Line's direction is most important, for in a large measure it controls the movements of our eyes while viewing a picture. This movement may bring about continuity of relationships among the various elements and their properties.

Location

The control exercised over the foregoing line properties may be enhanced or diminished by the *location* of the line. According to its placement, a line may serve to *unify* or *divide* and *balance* or *unbalance* a pictorial area. A diagonal line may be soaring or plunging depending on its high or low position relative to the frame. The various attributes of line may act in concert toward one goal or may be serving separate roles of expression and design. It is obvious, therefore, that a fully developed work may recognize and utilize all physical factors; although it is also possible that less than the total number may be successfully used. This is true largely because of the dual role of these properties. For instance, *unity* in a work may be achieved by *repetition* of line length while *variety* is being created by *difference* in its width, medium or other properties.

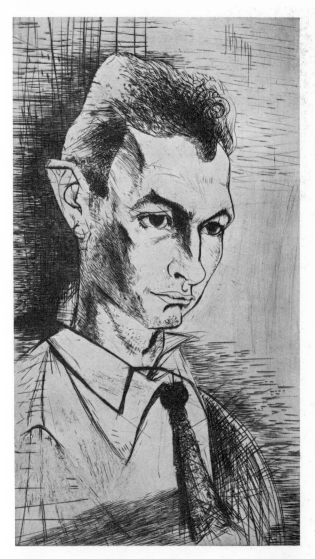

Figure 21. SELF PORTRAIT by James Steg. This engraving illustrates the wide applications of line; a *meeting* of *areas* where texture and values change (contrast between cross-hatching pattern of background and the white of hair), *contour* as it defines the edge of the face, and *enrichment* of the *surface as seen,* in many areas throughout the print.
Courtesy of the artist.

Character

Along with *measure, type, direction,* and *location,* line possesses *character,* a term largely related to the *medium* with which it is created. Different media or medium conditions may be used to create greater interest. Monotony could result from the consistent use of lines of the

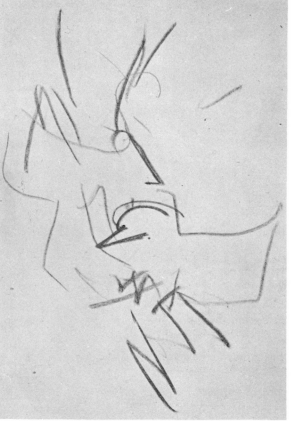

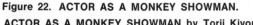

Figure 22. ACTOR AS A MONKEY SHOWMAN.

Figure 23. COCK FIGHT.

ACTOR AS A MONKEY SHOWMAN by Torii Kiyonobu. The alterations of movement in the *curved lines* of this Japanese print are visually entertaining because of their subtle rhythmical quality. The abrupt changes of direction in the *angular lines* of the student drawing of a *Cock Fight* create the excitement and tension of the combat.

Courtesy The Metropolitan Museum of Art, New York. Rogers Fund, 1936.

same character unless the unity so gained was balanced by the variation of other physical properties. The nature of the drawing instrument is important in determining the *emotional quality* of the line. One can easily see the different *expressive* qualities inherent in the soft, blurred lines of *chalk* as opposed to the precise and firm lines of *pen* and *ink*. Other instruments, *brush, burin, stick, fingers,* etc., all contain distinctive expressive capabilities which may be exploited by the artist. The artist is the real master of the situation, and it is his ability, experience, intention, and mental and physical condition that will determine the effectiveness of *line character*. According to the artist producing them, one may find lines of uniformity or ac-

cent, certainty or indecision, tension or relaxation.

EMOTIONAL OR EXPRESSIVE PROPERTIES OF LINE

The *emotional qualities* of line may be described by general states of feeling—gay, somber, tired, energetic, brittle, alive, etc. However, in a work of art as in the human mind, such feelings are rarely so clearly defined. There are an infinite number of emotional conditions of varying subtleties which may be communicated by the artist. The recognition of these qualities by the spectator is a matter of feeling, meaning that he must be receptive and perceptive and have his own reservoir of experiences.

Figure 24. LINE CHARAC-TER. A number of tools and media are found in this one drawing: brush-and-ink, pen and ink, chalk, pencil, matchstick, and ink. The variety of materials and their manipulation by the artist give expressive qualities to each individual figure.

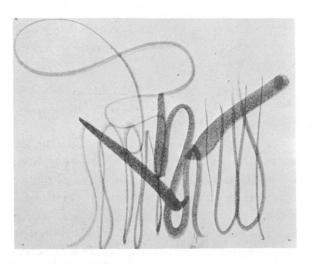

Figure 25. VIOLINIST.   **Figure 26. ORCHESTRA LEADER.**

EMOTIONAL QUALITY. There are a number of emotional qualities that can be created by the manner in which the artist varies the *line character*. The idea of *violinist* is expressed in one of these line groupings; the other represents an abstract concept of an *orchestra leader*.

One can enlarge quite extensively on the many uses of line in the work of art. Through the factors of *composition* and *expression,* individual lines come to life as they play their various roles. Some lines are dominant and some subordinate, but all are of supreme importance in a work of art. Although lines may be admired separately, their real beauty lies in the *relationships* which they help to establish, the *form* created. This form may be *representational* or *nonrepresentational,* but the recognition and the enjoyment of the work on the *abstract* level is of first importance. Primary preoccupation with subject identification will materially reduce the appreciation of the truly expressive art qualities.

LINE AS RELATED TO THE OTHER ART ELEMENTS

There are other physical properties of line which are so closely involved with the other art elements that they should be studied in terms of those relationships. Line may possess *color, value,* and *texture,* and it may create *shape.* Some of these factors are essential to the very creation of line while others may be introduced as needed. These properties may be thought of separately, but nevertheless they cooperate to give line an intrinsic appeal, meaning that line may be admired for its own sake. Artists often exploit this appeal by creating pictures in which the linear effects are dominant, the others subordinate.

Line and Shape
Colorplate 13

In creating *shape,* line serves as a continuous *edge* of a figure, object or mass. A line which describes an area in this manner is called *contour. Contour* may further operate as a separation between *shapes, values, textures,* and *colors.*

Colorplate 14

A series of closely placed lines create *textures* and *toned areas.* The relationships of the ends of these *linear areas* establish boundaries that transpose them into *shapes.*

Line and Value
The contrast in light and dark which a line exhibits against its background is termed *value.* Every line must demonstrate this quality in order to remain visible. This *value* may be the result of mixture or pressure depending on the *medium* being used. *Groups* of single lines create areas which show *value* differences. Parallel lines, hatchings, etc., are included in such groups.

Line and Texture
When groups of lines such as those mentioned combine to produce a flat or two-dimensional effect, *pattern* results. If, however, the result is one which stimulates our sensations of touch by suggesting degrees of roughness or smoothness, the effect may be termed *texture.* *Texture* also resides within the character of

Figure 27. A *contour* drawing when made without looking at the paper may create unexpected distortions which add *expressive* quality to the line produced.

various *media* and *tools* and gives them their distinctive qualities. Each tool possesses the *textural properties* of its structure and use, and these, in turn, may be enhanced or diminished by the manner of handling. Brushes of a hard bristle, for instance, can either make sharp or rough lines depending on hand pressure, *amount* of medium carried, and *quality* of execution. Brushes with soft hairs can produce smooth lines if loaded with thin paint and thick blotted lines if loaded with heavy paint. Other *tools* and *media* similarly produce variations of *line* in terms of the factors mentioned.

Line and Color

The introduction of *color* to a line adds a vast creative potential. Color may serve to *accent* or neutralize other line properties; a hard line combined with an *intense* color will produce a forceful or even harsh effect. This effect could be considerably overcome were the identical line created in a more gentle color. *Color* has become identified with various emotional states and may be used by the artist to apply them. For instance, red might symbolize passion or anger, yellow could suggest cowardice or warmth, etc.

Colorplate 15

Figure 28. The *plastic* quality of a shape may be produced by lines which move across and within the form as well as on its edge or *contour*.

Figure 29. In this student drawing, we find a series of closely placed parallel lines to indicate dark-and-light differences. This use of line gives a decorative quality to the entire drawing.

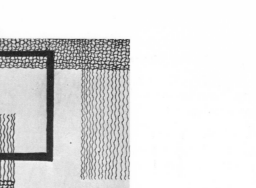

Figure 30. A classroom experiment in the creation of *texture* with pen and ink line. The similarity of the wavy lines used create a textural harmony throughout the *pattern*. The use of the heavy vertical-horizontal line and difference in value add interest through *contrast*.

SPATIAL CHARACTERISTICS OF LINE

All of the physical properties of line contain *spatial* ingredients which are subject to control by the artist. Mere position within a prescribed area suggests *space*. *Value contrast* may cause lines to advance and recede. An individual line which has varied *values* throughout its length may appear to writhe and twist in space. As in general, *warm* colors *advance* and *cool* colors *recede,* the *spatial properties* of colored lines are obvious. Every factor which produces *line* has something to say about its location in space. The artist's job is to use these factors to create *spatial order.*

LINE AND REPRESENTATION

Line creates *representation* on both *abstract* and *realistic* levels. In general, we have dealt primarily with abstract definitions, but it is easy to see that the application may be simultaneously observed in a material context. For example, we have mentioned the *advancing-receding* qualities of value in a line; if this particular line was one which had been drawn to represent the *contours* of a piece of drapery, we could see that *value contrast* might describe the relative *spatial* position of the folds of the drapery. A linear portrait of a person may utilize line properties to suggest more than its mere physical presence. It may contain much information on the character of the sitter. The artist may state this satirically or sympathetically. Thus, line in representation has many implications both objective and subjective. All of them are the direct result of the manipulation of the *physical properties* by the artist.

In their role of signifying ideas and conveying feelings, lines move and live, pulsating with significant emotions. In art, line becomes a means for transcribing the *graphic language* of ideas

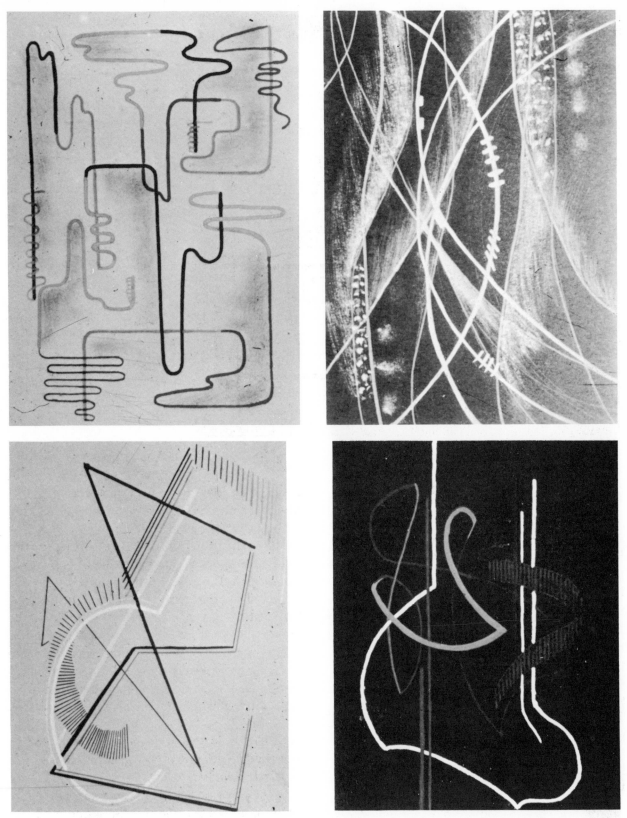

Figure 31. The varying *physical* properties of line used in these student experiments demonstrate *spatial* dimension on otherwise flat surfaces. The lines used vary in color, value, thickness, direction type, and location in space.

and emotions. It describes the edges or *contours* of shapes; it diagrams silhouettes; it encompasses spaces and areas; all done in such a way as to convey meaning.

Line is not used *exclusively* to express deep emotion and experience in this manner. Often, it is used for the planning of *utilitarian* objects— the line drawings of a building prepared by an architect or the drawings of a bridge made by an engineer—the lines drawn on maps to represent rivers, roads or contours—or the lines drawn on paper to represent words. Such use of line is primarily utilitarian, a convenient way of communicating ideas to another person. Whichever the emphasis, *expression* of human emotions or *communication* of factual materials, line is an important *plastic element* at the disposal of the artist.

Figure 32. PORTRAIT OF MAX JACOB by Juan Gris. Line can add *spatial dimension* to representative drawing. The accent and modulation of line used to describe this figure helps to give it a feeling of *plastic* quality.

Courtesy The Museum of Modern Art, New York. Gift of James Thrall Soby.

LINE PROBLEMS

PROBLEM 1

Line has infinite variety according to the medium used and the manipulation of that medium by the artist.

Cover a whole sheet of paper with lines using every medium which you have available. Strive for variety by manipulating the medium in every conceivable way.

PROBLEM 2

Lines may vary as to direction and position.

In frame shapes, create four interesting line patterns. One should be composed of vertical and horizontal lines only, one of diagonal lines, one of curved lines, and one of a combination of lines of all directions. Vary the length, thickness, spacing, and color of the lines so as to make the pattern interesting.

Figure 33.

PROBLEM 3

Lines may be balanced symmetrically or they may be balanced asymmetrically. When lines are paired equally on either side of a vertical axis they are balanced symmetrically. Lines may be different in terms of their physical properties and measures, but if they are equal in terms of their spatial fields an equilibrium will be reached on the picture plane. Such line balance is termed asymmetrical.

In a picture frame balance a group of lines symmetrically and asymmetrically. Vary the physical properties of the lines.

PROBLEM 4

Lines may be decorative or they may be spatial in character. When lines are of the same thickness and do not cross each other they tend to decorate a surface without giving any significant sense of space. If lines cross, vary in thickness, and are of different colors, they may express a plastic quality; that is, they may seem to exist in a three-dimensional or space relationship.

On a single sheet of paper, make two design patterns of lines, each contained within a frame shape. One should be a design in which the lines have a decorative effect and all seem to lie on the plane of the paper; the other should be made so that the lines seem to exist in space.

Figure 34.

PROBLEM 5

The artist may combine the decorative and the spatial characteristics of line within the same area.

Using three media create a continuous contour drawing of the edges of transparent objects such as bottles. Repeat the original contour in the other two media, enhancing the decorative nature of the contours. In addition, draw the ellipses forming the mouths and bottoms of the bottles, and overlap the bottles in such a way that the contour lines of those in back are allowed to come through those in front, thus enhancing the overall spatial character of the bottles.

Figure 35.

PROBLEM 6

The kind of line used may express emotional qualities. Straight lines are rigid, diagonal lines are exciting, vertical lines are dignified, horizontal lines are quiet and restful, etc.

Express three emotions in abstract line patterns developed within a design field. Name each emotion.

Figure 36.

PROBLEM 7

The form of an object may be expressed in one continuous line and the form will take on qualities of expression depending on the medium used.

Draw several objective forms in a continuous line using the potentialities of the medium. With crayons vary the lightness and darkness of the line; with brush and ink vary the thickness and thinness of the line. Try ink lines on damp paper. Try pencil using a broad stroke with the side of the pencil. Use lines with paint applied thickly as well as thinned with water.

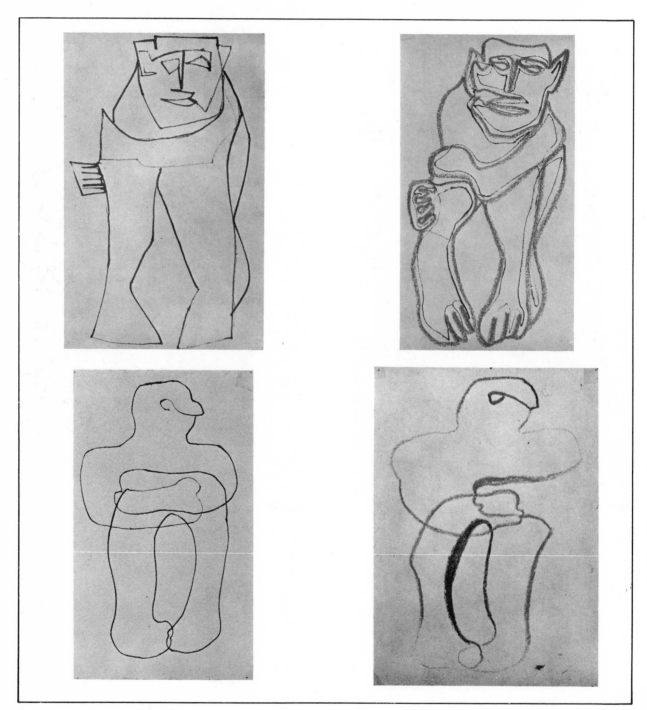

Figure 37.

PROBLEM 8

Lines may describe the boundaries of object-shapes.

Concentrating the eye on the outer edge of an object, follow the contour with a drawing instrument. When the drawing is completed vary the lines for spatial and emotional effects.

PROBLEM 9

Single lines when grouped create areas of dark and light.

Draw parallel lines across the breadth of represented objects, varying the spaces between the lines to produce changes of value.

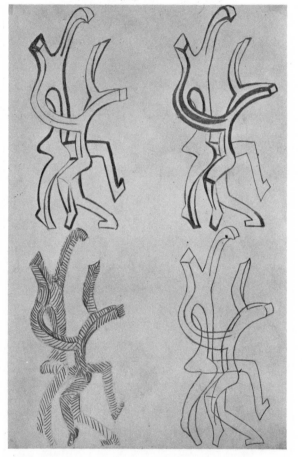

Figure 38.

Figure 39.

CHAPTER 5: SHAPE

Definitions:

Shape: An area which stands out from the space next to or around it because of a defined boundary or because of a difference of value, color, or texture.

Decorative shapes: Those shapes which are two-dimensional in nature and seem to lie flat on the surface of the picture plane.

Plane: A shape which is essentially two-dimensional in nature but whose relationships with other shapes may give an illusion of a third dimension.

Volume: A shape which is three-dimensional in nature and exists in space. On a flat surface the artist can only create the *illusion* of a volume.

Geometric shapes: Those shapes created by the exact mathematical laws of geometry. They are usually simple in character such as the triangle, the rectangle, the circle.

Rectilinear shapes: Shapes whose boundaries usually consist entirely of straight lines.

Biomorphic shapes: Usually more or less irregular shapes which resemble the freely developed curves found in live organisms.

Cubism: A term given to the artistic style which uses mostly geometric shapes, usually two-dimensional in nature.

Surrealism: A style of artistic expression which emphasizes fantasy and whose subjects are usually the experiences revealed by the subconscious mind.

Linear perspective: A mechanical system for creating the illusion of a three-dimensional space on a two-dimensional surface.

Shapes are of much the same importance to the artist as bricks to the bricklayer. Both represent the materials from which can be fashioned structures of beauty, craftsmanship, and permanence. However, bricks are *tangible objects*, whereas shapes exist primarily in terms of *the illusion which they create*. The artist's role is to use the illusionistic property of this element of shape so as to lend credence to the fantasy which is inherent in his art. The illusion created may be one of *pure fantasy* developed along non-representative lines. It may be a *semifantasy* in which the artist originates his work with identifiable objects but enhances their aspects in order to create a unified expression. If the creator is a capable artist, the eventual form, regardless of its *degree of fantasy*, can be perfectly convincing as a *type of reality*. *Reality* in this case obviously surpasses mere *description*, unless our definition of description is enlarged to include the world of imagination.

DEFINITION OF SHAPE

If one must define it, a *shape* may be called an area of *value, color, line*, or all three, possessing more or less measurable dimensions. Its dimensions are only occasionally measurable, because it may be of great delicacy or complexity; it may be gradually blended with other shapes so that the relationship renders their areas practically indistinguishable. *Shape variety* is without limit, ranging from symmetrical

Figure 40. ANIMALS by Rufino Tamayo. In "Animals" Tamayo has conjured up beasts animal-like in general appearance but unclassifiable as to any recognizable species. These animals have been purged of all domestication, emphasizing their primitive savagery. The stark environment aids in the development of this expression which, visually speaking, has no exact parallel in nature but which seems perfectly reasonable as an expression of elemental brutishness.

Courtesy The Museum of Modern Art, New York. Inter-American Fund.

to asymmetrical, poised to awkward, static to dynamic, outgoing to retiring, and so on, ad infinitum.

USE OF SHAPES

Shapes, in works of art, may be readily recognized as representing known objects, but we cannot necessarily assume this fact to be the artist's *primary concern.* The observer rarely knows the exact nature of the physical objects from which the artist's work derives; as a result, he cannot assess the *degree* of devotion to *actual appearances* as shown by the work. Usually the *subject-objects* are the origins of a "feeling" or train of thought in the artist's mind; this then becomes a personal expression which cannot be portrayed through the *literal copying* of surface appearances. Object-shapes, therefore, undergo a certain transformation (of varying degrees) and become individualized as a part of the *style or language* of the artist. Sometimes, this

Colorplate
16

Figure 41. MAUSOLEUM.

Figure 42. MAUSOLEUM.

Object shapes often undergo a considerable transformation according to the individual manner of the artist. Such a transformation is illustrated in the comparison between a photograph and the print of a mausoleum. The object, as such, was not so important as the final art form.

transformation develops shapes which are *totally unlike* those seen in nature. This demonstrates that the *object,* as such, is not so important to the artist as is the final viewpoint.

The final art form is to be reached under the discipline of certain fundamental principles of composition which control and direct the *ordering of shapes* as well as the other *elements of form.* Under these principles, the elements share responsibility for:

1. The achievement of balance.
2. The control of the direction and duration of the observer's attention.
3. The development of an appropriate ratio between harmony (repetition) and variety.
4. The consistency of space concept.

Each of these principles is of such importance as to merit some individual study.

Balance

In seeking compositional balance, consideration must be given the *amounts of force* or weight symbolized by shapes. The teeter-totter may be used as an analogy in this respect; by placing shapes of various sizes at different distances from the fulcrum, it becomes obvious that the apparent balance of the apparatus is subject to control. In this instance (as in all pictorial balancing) the sense of weight is *intuitive* or "felt" in the art elements in terms of the various properties composing them. For instance, a dark shape "seems" heavier, or a shape with intense color "seems" to have a stronger attraction. The example of the teeter-totter

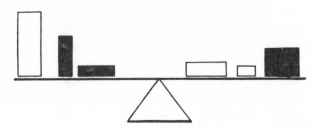

Figure 43. Diagram showing *amounts of force* or weight symbolized by shapes, using a teeter-totter as an analogy.

given us a vision of a completely alien milieu. Though as far as imaginable from everyday reality this environment seems, if not likely, at least possible, thanks to the facility of the artist.

Courtesy The Museum of Modern Art, New York.

Colorplate 17. THE MEETING OF SAINT ANTHONY AND SAINT PAUL by Sassetta and Assistant. In this painting by the Renaissance artist Sassetta "station stops" of varied duration are indicated by contrasts of value. In
addition "eye-paths" are provided by the edges of the natural forms which lead from figure to figure.

Courtesy The National Gallery of Art, Washington, D.C. Samuel H. Kress Collection.

Colorplate 18. THE BLUE WINDOW by Henri Matisse. Matisse has abstracted organic forms for the purpose of decorative organization rather than symbolic meanings or intentions.

Colorplate 19. THE ADORATION OF THE SHEPHERDS by Giorgione. Giorgione reflects the period of the early 16th-century when the concept of space was primarily concerned with the illusion of boundlessness. Although many present-day artists favor a shallow space, some retain the interminable concept.

Colorplate 20. PHIPPSBURG, MAINE by John Marin. John Marin may be cited as an example of a present-day artist who prefers to emphasize the essential flatness of his painting surface. He does this by limiting his space.

Courtesy The Metropolitan Museum of Art, The Alfred Stieglitz Collection.

Colorplate 21. THREE WOMEN (LE GRAND DEJEUNER) by Fernand Léger. Léger often used sharply defined shape edges which act as barriers or fences to temporarily halt eye travel. However, in order to avoid complete isolation of shapes, the artist uses basic interval, shape direction, and variation in strength of shape edges to encourage unity and visual passage.

Collection The Museum of Modern Art, New York. Mrs. Simon Guggenheim Fund.

Figure 44.
Courtesy National Gallery of Art, Washington, D.C. Chester Dale Collection.

STILL LIFE: THE TABLE by Georges Braque. The painting by the French cubist, Georges Braque, has many elements which contain directions of force. The diagram with the simplified grouping of dark illustrates the controlled tensions resulting from the placement, size, accent, and general character of the shapes used by the artist. The white arrows show the predetermined eye paths by which the artist creates visual transition and rhythmic movement.

Figure 45.

demonstrates force along *one axis only*; this becomes very elementary when we consider that a pictorial area may contain *many elements* of many *directions* of force. The direction and amounts of force depend on *placement, size, accent,* and *general shape character* (including associational equivalents). The *amounts of force* developing out of all these factors should counterbalance each other so that a *controlled tension* results.

Colorplate
17

Control of Attention direction

The momentum generated by this use of shapes leads to the possibility of *controlled vision*. The artist may guide the attention of the observer according to certain predetermined paths. This facilitates *visual transition* from one area to another and opens the way for the use of *rhythmic movement*, the rhythm serving as an effective unifying device.

Figure 46. Examination of this *Crucifixion* by Otto Ocvirk reveals that the artist has made the figure of Christ paramount primarily through location, size, and value contrast.

duration or relative dominance

The creation of related directions serving to bind together the optical units of a work of art is not enough for a complete aesthetic expression. One would hardly care to take a trip if the itinerary did not include scheduled stops or "breaks" in the monotony of the drive. The length of time involved in these pauses are ordinarily planned according to the significance of the locations to be viewed; so it is with the planning of a work of art. The determination of the importance of the various areas of the work is a matter of artistic selection; it results from the influence of *design principles* as well as the *artist's feelings* about his subject matter. Examination of a picture of the crucifixion, for example, would probably reveal that the artist had somehow managed to make the figure of Christ paramount in pictorial importance. Importance of this kind would be based on contrast of *location, size, value, texture,* or *color.* The *degree of contrast* is determined by the amount of spectator attention desired.

This principle of *shape dominance* operates in both representational and non-representational work, but it is tempered to some extent by qualities of association. An oval shape in a non-representational painting might inherit more than its desired degree of importance if we were to interpret it as being a head. Such interpretation as this is usually personal and cannot always be foreseen by the artist. Whenever possible, the innate appeal of *associational factors* is used to advantage by the artist; these factors are weighed in the balance of *relative dominance* and forced to operate to the benefit of the *total organization.*

Shape Character

The qualities which relate or differentiate shapes may be the product of technique or inherent *shape character.* In a broad sense, shape character may be *natural* as when it seems to be a product of the vitality of nature (in stones, leaves, puddles, clouds, etc.), or it may be *abstract* when it is apparently contrived by the artist. The distinction between these two aspects is not always easily determined, for the variations of both *natural* and *man-made* shapes are vast indeed. Generally speaking, we tend to think of natural forms as those which have been molded and shaped by the forces of nature into rounded shapes. The most elemental organic forms encountered in biological study (amoebas, viruses, cells, internal organs) are preeminently rounded or curvilinear. This biological affinity for the curve has led to the term, *biomorphic,* to describe those curvilinear shapes in art which suggest the possibility of life.

Biomorphic shapes have developed considerable significance, particularly in the hands of the surrealist artists. This shape exploitation by the surrealists is no coincidence, for their interests include the mystic origins of being and the explorations of subconscious revelations, as in dreams. Other artists (such as Matisse) have *abstracted* organic forms in a less symbolic and primarily decorative manner.

In direct contrast to *biomorphic shapes* are the *rectilinear* or straight line, geometric, shapes. These generally seem to bear the precisionistic imprint of man's invention. The use of such shapes, as we know them today, was given its original impetus in the cubist design tradition. These shapes are inherently rigid and strong; and, when welded together by the artist's instincts, form an enduring and sometimes impersonal design.

Biomorphic and rectilinear shapes are illustrative of *shape families*; they manifest *intrinsic qualities* endearing them to certain artists because they harmonize with the feelings and objectives of those artists. Obviously, there is a limitless range of shape types between the two extremes mentioned. No artist will arbitrarily reject a shape because he considers it the property of an alien style. There is no test of a shape but its successful admission to the work of art; if it "works," it is kept, if not, the search must be continued.

Colorplate 18

Shapes and Space
pictorial depth

Every work of art contains actual or implied shapes and, along with these, some degree of

Figure 47. MAMA, PAPA IS WOUNDED! by Yves Tanguy. Surrealists such as Yves Tanguy
have given considerable symbolic significance to biomorphic shapes. They remind one of
basic organic matter, or flowing and changing shapes in dreams.

Courtesy The Museum of Modern Art, New York. Purchase.

space. Artists throughout history have reflected the controlling concepts of their times in their use of *pictorial space*. According to these concepts, the spatial phenomena became decoratively flat, shallow, or illusionistically infinite. The last hundred years have witnessed the transition from *deep space* to the *shallow space* favored by many present-day artists. This preference is exhibited today because of the feeling that shallow space permits greater *organization-*

al control of the art elements and is more in keeping with the essential flatness of the working surface. However, *all* spatial concepts are amply in evidence today, giving an indication of the diversity of our contemporary art scene. Space concepts are used arbitrarily, and even in combination, when necessary to achieve the desired results.

Colorplate
19

volumes and planes

The creation of three-dimensional shapes (*volumes* or *masses*) automatically implies the depth of space within which they must exist. The component *planes* (sides) of these volumes may be detached from their mother volume and inclined back into space at any angle and to any depth. They may also be presented *frontally* (parallel to the picture plane) creating an illusion of finely graded differences of depth within a shallow space. The essential difference between a *plane* and a *volume* lies in the absence of thickness in the *plane*. The plane is therefore less substantial and more flexible in its exploration of space.

Colorplate
20

Figure 48. GUITAR AND FLOWERS by Juan Gris. In direct contrast to biomorphic shapes are rectilinear or straight line shapes preferred by the cubists. Such shape families as the biomorphic and rectilinear are used by artists to unify, through repetition, their picture surface.

Courtesy The Museum of Modern Art, New York. Bequest of Anne Erickson Levene in memory of her husband, Dr. Phoebus Aaron Theodor Levene.

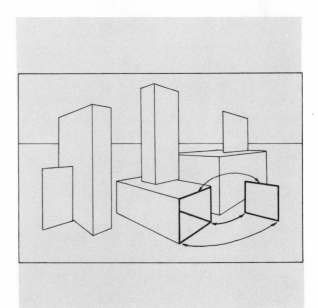

Figure 49. A drawing showing the essential difference between planes and volumes. Planes are shapes having only two dimensions (height and width); whereas volumes which are made up of planes have the effect of solidity or three dimensions (height, width, and depth). The component planes (sides) of volumes may be detached and inclined back in space at any angle as indicated by the arrows in the drawing.

intuitive space

Planes and volumes may be treated in terms of *linear perspective*, the illusionistic spatial technique whose effects are most commonly recognized. They may also be controlled in accordance with the artist's desire to create a space termed *intuitive*, implying that space is sensed or "felt" in the pictorial area. This type of space has been in evidence during much of the history of man's art. It follows no mechanical rules or formulae and is unique with each work of art. *Intuitive* methods of space control include overlapping, transparency, interpenetration, inclined planes, disproportionate scale, fractional representation, and any application of the inherent *spatial properties* of the art elements (such as advancing and receding properties of *color, value, texture,* etc.).

Figure 50. VIADUCT by Lyonel Feininger. In this painting the artist has used *intuitive* (or suggested) methods of space control including overlapping planes, transparencies, and planes that interpenetrate one another and incline into space. There are also some indications of disproportionate scale and fractional representation.

Courtesy The Museum of Modern Art, New York. Acquired through the Lillie P. Bliss bequest.

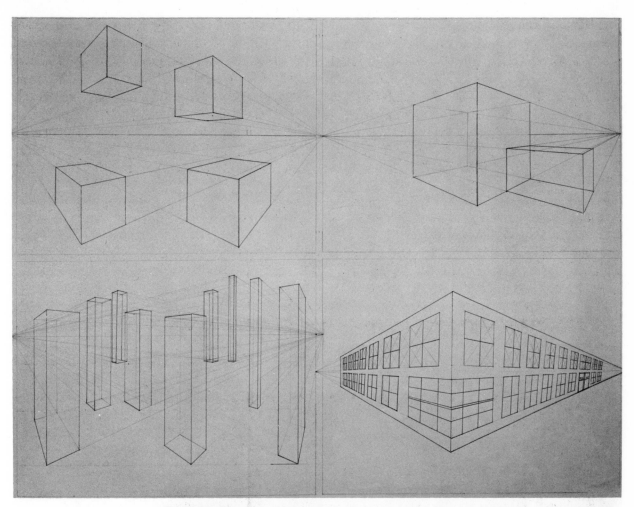

Figure 51. Examples of planes and volumes developed through the use of linear perspective, the spatial technique which creates the illusion of unconfined space. The illusion of space with this approach to drawing is based on the location of the artist in reference to the objects drawn and is accomplished by directing parallel lines toward a common point (an eye level or horizon) related to that location.

linear perspective

Linear perspective is a mechanical means of demonstrating the visual appearance of planes and volumes in space. This appearance is based on the location of the artist in reference to the objects drawn; it is accomplished by directing parallel lines toward a common point related to that location. This method of space development has been most popular during periods of scientific inquiry, culminating in the mid-nineteenth century. Despite the seeming virtue of its agreement with natural appearances, there are certain disadvantages pertaining to its application in art; these, in the opinion of many artists, outweigh its usefulness. Briefly, its liabilities are:

1. It is never an honest statement of actual shape or volume as it is *known* to be.

2. The only appearances which can be legitimately portrayed are those which can be seen by the artist observer from his one position in space.

3. The necessary recession of parallel lines toward common points often leads to monotonous visual effects.

4. The shape distortion created by perspective decreases the design areas available to the artist.

These disadvantages are quoted only to suggest that *familiar modes of vision* are not necessarily those which function best in a *work of art*.

Shape Edges

Colorplate
21

The border or edge of a shape is of considerable importance despite its frequent neglect by the artist. In the definition of a shape, we pointed out that a border is unnecessary as the extremities of *value* or *texture* are frequently sufficient to describe its limits. The most obvious conception of shape, however, consists of an *outlined area*. If the outline is very heavy, it can isolate shapes from each other, and repeated outlining of this kind may create a cha-

otic situation, with the strong lines creating roadblocks for the eyes. To avert this danger, the artist may utilize the basic interval and direction of the shapes to create unity; or, he may *control* contour strength in such a way as to encourage *visual passage* through the work. On the other hand, some artists deliberately choose to work with hazy, indistinct shapes; they, in turn, must realize that such shapes may be handled so as to preserve this softened character, but each area must count as a design shape.

Figure 52. LISTEN TO LIVING (Ecoutez Vivre) by Matta. This surrealistic painting by Matta, on the other hand, demonstrates the gradual blending of shapes which become indistinct and no longer measurable. Such shapes by their softened, flowing character provide a self-acting integration of parts.

Courtesy The Museum of Modern Art, New York. Inter-American Fund.

Formal Meaning of Shape

All of the principles involved in ordering shapes are of little avail if those shapes are barren of suggesting or *meaning*. Of course, the fullness of *shape meaning* can only be revealed through the relationships developed by the language of art. Nevertheless, there are certain meanings within shapes, some readily recognizable, others more complex and less clear. Some common meanings ascribable to *square*, for example, might be perfection, stability, stolidity, symmetry, self-reliance, or monotony. *Squares* may have different meanings for different people, but the number of meanings which could find general agreement are ample evidence of the common sensations shared when viewing a shape. Similarly, circles, ovals, rectangles, and a vast array of other shapes possess distinctive meanings; their meaningfulness depends on their *complexity*, their application, and the *sensitivity of those observing them*. The artist usually selects his shapes according to the *expression* he wishes to project, but he may be *initially* motivated by the psychological suggestions of shape. Such suggestions are exploited by psychologists in the familiar ink blot tests which are designed to aid in the evaluation of emotional stability. The mere existence of the test points up the fact that shapes can provoke *emotional responses* on different levels. Thus, the artist may use *abstract* shapes to create desired responses. By using his knowledge that some shapes are inevitably associated with certain objects and situations, he can set the stage for his pictorial drama.

Picture Frame as a Shape

Finally, the very surface on which the artist works is a shape, the *frame* or perimeter around it creating the border. In accordance with principles already mentioned, this *frame shape* presents the germ of a mood, depending upon its *degree of rectangularity*. Horizontal shapes should predominate in a horizontal frame and vertical shapes in a vertical frame. This creates a basic harmony *between the frame and its contents* and emphasizes the mood of the original shape.

Figure 53. THE EAST WIND by Charles Burchfield. The shapes used by Burchfield in this painting are partly psychological and partly symbolic. These shapes suggest the qualities of an approaching spirit-ridden storm.

Courtesy The Museum of Modern Art, New York. Gift of Mrs. W. Murray Crane.

SHAPE PROBLEMS

PROBLEM 1

Every artist starts with one large shape (the frame shape); his problem is how to divide or break up this area into smaller shapes which are interesting in themselves as well as in their relationships to each other.

With a crayon divide a rectangular shape into five or six areas of unequal size and varied in shape character. Strive for variety but keep some areas simple enough to avoid overcomplexity. Make several experiments of this kind; then select the one most satisfying and fill the areas in with solid color of contrasting tones. Try to make the most interesting shapes stand out through a contrast of value and/or color.

Figure 54.

PROBLEM 2

Shapes which lie on the surface of the picture plane are called decorative shapes and merely divide the plane into pattern. Shapes which are overlapping divide the space but also create a feeling of depth. Such shapes are called planes and may create movements back and forth in space.

Divide your rectangular shape with overlapping planes. Try to create a movement backwards into space but not so deep that the unity of the pattern with the picture plane is destroyed. Create variations by changing the sizes of the planes and placing them into different spatial relationships to the original picture surface. Have enough similarity in the plane shapes so that they can be considered to belong to the same shape families. Variations could be made by overlapping transparent planes so that new shapes are created.

Figure 55.

PROBLEM 3

In seeking compositional balance, we must recognize that shapes represent moments of force. The moments or attractions between shapes must counterbalance one another.

Balance and counterbalance several geometric shapes within the boundaries of a picture frame. Consider these shapes as forces which should support one another in a controlled tension. Add value and color to the shapes to create interest. Remember that changes of color, value, and texture can affect the weight as well as size and variety of shapes.

PROBLEM 4

Shape families represent relationships of areas through the sharing of common qualities.

Create three decorative organizations using:
a. Rectangular shapes which are vertical and horizontal to frame the border.
b. Triangular shapes.
c. Biomorphic shapes.

PROBLEM 5

The space concept used with shapes may be shallow, deep, or infinite. Circles, squares, and triangles are basic two-dimensional shapes; spheres, cubes, pyramids, cones, and cylinders are basic three-dimensional shapes.

   a. Arrange several circles, squares, and triangles in decorative and in a shallow space.

   b. Transform this into deep space by substituting in a second arrangement solid forms such as cubes, pyramids, etc.

Figure 56.

PROBLEM 6

All shapes do not have definite borders but may subtly blend one into the other; likewise, some shapes may be defined by a borderline only, without a change of value and color.

Using chalk, divide or break up a rectangular space with patches of color. Rub or blend some of these color shapes together so that they lose their distinct edges. Introduce into this design some linear shapes; use some lines to redefine or reaccent areas and superimpose some new linear pattern shapes.

Figure 57.

PROBLEM 7

Shapes which contrast in value are much more dominant in pattern than those which are defined with a linear border only. Such shapes, if large, tend to unify several smaller line shapes.

Make an outline drawing from a complex still-life group. In this drawing, shapes may be simplified rather than having all of the naturalistic details indicated. Using any shading medium, create several large tone shapes by combining a number of the smaller outlined forms. Slight variations of tone or texture may be used within these larger shapes to indicate significant details. In addition, certain shapes which might be considered important may be stressed by making bolder and heavier the original outline which defined them.

Figure 58.

PROBLEM 8

The principles of linear perspective may be used to create spatial effects with shape volumes.

Starting with simple geometric solids whose sides are parallel (cubes, rectangular solids) organize the spatial characteristics of a picture field through the perspective of these volumes. Place some solids above and below the horizon, some in which the base is on the ground plane and the top is above the horizon.

This problem may be followed by one which uses more complex volumes based on cylinders, cones, and spheres.

Figure 59.

PROBLEM 9

Shapes may be used to portray natural objects in many different ways. Such shapes frequently undergo a transformation (distortion) in order to strengthen a pictorial design.

Set up and arrange a group of still-life objects. Draw the object-shapes as seen in this arrangement from a fixed position. Pay particular attention to the sizes, proportions, and the positive-negative shape relationships. Use lines and value changes to portray these object-shapes (an approach to naturalism).

In a second picture, draw and rearrange the same still-life group. Flatten the object-shapes and spaces to create a decorative pictorial pattern. Sacrifice objective identity in order to unify this pictorial organization.

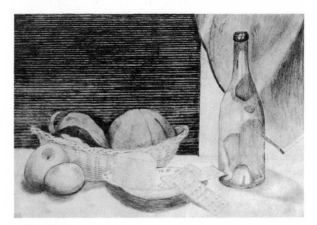

Figure 60a.

Figure 60b.

PROBLEM 10

Like line, shapes of various kinds can suggest emotional or expressive qualities.

a. Working with either free, geometric, or with combinations of shape families, create abstract expressions for such titles as *Tempest, Rowers, Strikers, Ballet Dancers, Circus Clowns,* etc.

b. Try the same thing using invented words such as *Balooma, Irskt, Sleema, Rz-z-z-z-z, Sloovonious,* etc.

c. Try to express your own reactions to certain situations such as *loneliness, mystery, excitement, triumph, despair, conflict,* etc.

Figure 61a.

PROBLEM 11

For pictorial unity, it is recommended that we use shapes which will echo or repeat the basic character of the picture frame (frame shape).

Select a real object with fairly complex and interesting outline forms. Use one which might be assumed to have normal or average proportions. Draw and distort the object to fill and repeat the lines of:

a. An elongated vertical frame shape.
b. An exaggerated or stretched-out horizontal frame shape.

Figure 61b.

CHAPTER 6: VALUE

Definitions:

Value: The relative degree of lightness or darkness given to an area by the amount of light reflected from it.

Value Pattern: The total effect of the relationships of light and dark given to areas within the pictorial field.

1. *Two-dimensional*: Value relationships in which the changes of light and dark seem to occur only on the surface of the picture plane.
2. *Three-dimensional*: The value relationships which are planned to create an illusion of objects existing in depth back of the picture plane.

Decorative Value: A term given to a two-dimensional value pattern. It usually refers to areas of dark or light definitely confined within boundaries rather than the gradual blending of tones.

Chiaroscuro: A technique of representation which concentrates on the effects of blending the light and shade on objects to create the illusion of space or atmosphere.

Tenebrism: A style of painting which exaggerates or emphasizes the effects of chiaroscuro. Larger amounts of dark value are placed close to smaller areas of highly contrasting lights in order to concentrate the attention on certain important features.

Highlight: The area of a represented shape which receives the greatest amount of direct light.

Shadow: The dark area created on a surface when another form is placed so as to prevent the light from falling on that surface.

Shade, Shading: The darker value on the surface of a form which gives the illusion that it is turned away from the imagined source of light.

Local Value: The natural or characteristic value of a shape which is determined by its normal color independent from any effect created by the degree of light falling on it.

The visual experiences encountered in the plastic and graphic arts may be divided into two classes: *chromatic* (reds, greens, yellows, and other hues) and *achromatic* (white, black, and the limitless series of greys between white and black). There is nothing divisive about *value* itself, however, as it is an integral part of both chromatic and achromatic appearances. Value is variously termed *tone*, *brightness*, *shade*, or even *color*. Some of these terms, as we shall see, have only limited convenience and accuracy when considered in an *art* context. Perhaps the best definition for our purpose is that found in the dictionary, which states that value may be defined as "the relation of one part or detail in a picture to another with respect to lightness and darkness."[1]

RELATIONSHIP TO THE OTHER ART ELEMENTS

The student who is investigating art in its constituent parts must consider the relationships of *value* to the other elements of art form: *line*, *color*, *texture*, and *shape*. All of these elements

---

[1]Webster, N., Merriam, *Webster's Collegiate Dictionary*, 5th ed., G. & C. Merriam Co., Springfield, Mass., 1941 p. 1105.

must exhibit some value contrast with the material on which they are placed in order to remain visible.

The particular value manifested by a line could be the result of medium or the pressure exerted on the medium by the artist. For example, depending on the degree of hardness of a pencil you would create a dark or lighter tone, or line. Value may be created by a merger of elements, as when a number of lines of the same or different qualities are placed alongside or across each other to produce generalized *areas of value*. Shapes are therefore created and distinguished from each other by the use of value. Reproduction of textures relies on the values in the shadows and highlights peculiar to a particular type of surface, while abstract textures contain more or less flat lines and shapes of different values. The intoxicating effects of a color often blind people to the fact that the very existence of color is entirely dependent on the presence of value. A standard yellow, for

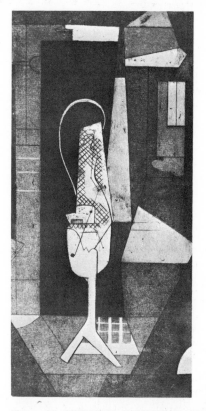

Figure 63. SPECTRAL INTERIOR by Philip Wigg. The print is a black-and-white picture, void of color, yet presenting a completely satisfying aesthetic statement.

Courtesy of the artist.

Figure 62. WOMEN WINDING WOOL by Henry Moore. In this drawing we have an example of the use of values to create the illusion of volumes and textures.

Courtesy The Museum of Modern Art, New York. Gift of Mr. and Mrs. John A. Pope in honor of Paul J. Sachs.

example, is of a far greater lightness than a standard violet although they may be modified to the point at which they become virtually equal. A common weakness in painting is the unfortunate disregard of the pattern created by *the value relationships* of the color; black-and-white photographs of paintings often reveal this deficiency very clearly. On the other hand, black-and-white pictures without benefit of color are traditional, commonplace, and may be perfectly satisfying as works of art. The application of value to the other art elements creates *two-dimensional pattern*, *accent*, and *spatial variation*. A good example of a two-dimensional pattern is a checkerboard. Generally, black and white areas will feature examples of accent and spatial variation.

Colorplate
22

DESCRIPTIVE USES OF VALUE

One of the most generally useful applications of value is found in its description of objects, shapes, and space. Descriptive qualities may be broadened to include psychological, emotional or dramatic expression. Artists from time immemorial have been concerned with value as a problem in translating light as it plays about the earth and its inhabitants. Objects are usually perceived in terms of the characteristic patterns which occur when the mass is exposed to light rays. Objects, at least according to customary occurrence, cannot receive light from all directions simultaneously. "A solid object will receive more light from one side than another because that side is closer to the light source and thus will intercept the light and cast shadows on the other side."[2]

Light patterns vary according to the *surface* of the object receiving the light. A *spherical surface* demonstrates this in an even flow from light to dark. An *angular surface* shows sudden contrasts of light and dark values. Each basic form has a basic highlight and shadow pattern. An evenly flowing tone-gradation invokes a sense of gently curved surface. An abrupt change of tone we translate as meaning a sharp or angular surface.[3]

Cast shadows are the dark areas which occur on an object when a shape is interposed between it and the light source. The nature of the shadow created depends, scientifically speaking, on the size and location of the light source, the size and shape of the interposed body, and the character of the forms on which the shadows fall. Although cast shadows give very definite clues to the circumstances of a given situation, they only occasionally give an ideal indication of the true nature of the forms. The artist normally uses, reuses, or *creates* those shadows which aid in descriptive character, enhance the effectiveness of the design pattern, and/or contribute substantially to the mood or expression.

Figure 64. A solid object will receive more light from one side than another because that side is closer to the light source and thus will intercept the light and cast shadows on the other side.

Figure 65. A photograph illustrating the even gradation of light to dark on a spherical surface and the sudden contrast of light and dark on an angular surface.

[2]Kepes, Gyorgy, *The Language of Vision*, Paul Theobald & Co., Chicago, 1951, p. 43.
[3]Ibid. p. 143.

Colorplate 22. DOG AND COCK by Pablo Picasso. The contemporary artist (such as Picasso) often uses abstract textures which may depend on the use of value but not for the purpose of description. Values indicating abstract textures, such as the linear or geometric symbols of "Dog and Cock" are used for compositional purposes such as variety, accent, or emphasis.

Colorplate 23. CHRIST AT THE SEA OF GALILEE by Tintoretto. Tintoretto commonly employs a preponderance of dark values interspersed with flickering lights to create an atmosphere of religious drama.

Courtesy The National Gallery of Art, Washington, D.C. Samuel H. Kress Collection.

Colorplate 24. THE CALLING OF THE APOSTLES PETER AND ANDREW by Duccio. Although line and shape predominate in Duccio's works, some of the early attempts at modelling with chiaroscuro value can be seen.

Courtesy The National Gallery of Art, Washington, D.C. Samuel H. Kress Collection.

Colorplate 25. THE ENTOMBMENT OF CHRIST by Titian *(copy of)*. The great Venetian, Titian, subordinated line, contrasting edges with value and enveloped his figures in a tonal atmosphere that approaches tenebrism.

Courtesy The Detroit Institute of Arts, Detroit, Michigan. Gift of James E. Scripps.

Colorplate 26. THE DESCENT FROM THE CROSS by Rembrandt van Rijn. Rembrandt often used inventive, implied, light sources that deviated from standard light conditions in order to enhance the mood or emotional expression.

Courtesy The National Gallery of Art, Washington, D.C. Widener Collection.

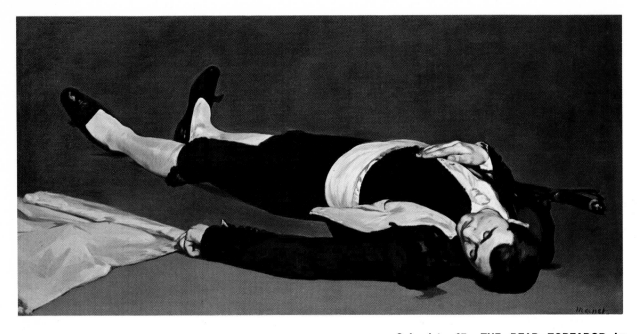

Colorplate 27. THE DEAD TOREADOR by Edouard Manet. Manet, a 19th-century naturalist, was one of the first artists to break with traditional chiaroscuro employing instead flat areas of value. These flat areas meet abruptly in comparison to the blended edges used by artists previous to Manet. This was one of the basic technical advances of 19th-century art.

Courtesy The National Gallery of Art, Washington, D.C. Widener Collection.

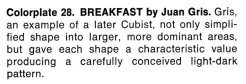

Colorplate 28. BREAKFAST by Juan Gris. Gris, an example of a later Cubist, not only simplified shape into larger, more dominant areas, but gave each shape a characteristic value producing a carefully conceived light-dark pattern.

Courtesy The Museum of Modern Art, New York. Lillie P. Bliss Bequest.

Figure 66. Light from an uncontrolled source may cast overlapping shadows which tend to break up and hide the true character of object forms. The unplanned shapes of shadows such as these will often disorganize compositional unity.

EXPRESSIVE USES OF VALUE

The type of expression sought by the artist ordinarily determines the balance between light and shadow in a work of art. It should be obvious that a preponderance of dark areas will create an atmosphere of gloom, mystery, drama, or menace, whereas a composition which is basically light will produce quite the opposite effect. Artists will tend to avoid *exact duplication* of cause and effect in light and shadow, because such a procedure would create a series of forms which are monotonously light or dark on the same side. The shapes of highlights and shadows are often revised to create desired degrees of unity and contrast with adjacent compositional areas. In summary, lights and shadows exist *in nature* as the by-products of strictly physical laws; the artist must adjust and take liberties with them in order to create his own visual language.

Figure 67. THE NOSTALGIA OF THE INFINITE by Giorgio de Chirico. Giorgio de Chirico often uses shadow effects, strong contrasts of value, and stark shapes to enhance the lonely, timeless nostalgia that is so much a part of his poetic expression.

Courtesy The Museum of Modern Art, New York. Purchase.

Chiaroscuro

Colorplate
23

Chiaroscuro is a word closely related to value and used frequently in art terminology. The term refers to the technique of representation which displays an obvious use of contrasting lights and darks. "Since the days of Leonardo da Vinci the term refers to the way the painter handles those atmospheric effects which permit him to create the illusion that his subjects are on all sides surrounded by space, letting them stand free."[4] The development of *chiaroscuro* in painting can be traced from Giotto· (1276-1335) who used darks and lights for modeling, but expressed shape and space in terms of line.

Colorplate
24

Masaccio, Fra Angelico, and Pollaiulo, the early Florentine masters, carried *chiaroscuro* a step farther by expressing the structure and volume in space with an even, graded tonality. Leonardo da Vinci employed a much bolder series of contrasts in light and dark but always with soft value transitions. The great Venetian painters such as Giorgione, Titian, and Tintoretto completely subordinated line, suggesting compositional unity through an enveloping atmosphere of dominant tonality.

---

[4]Runes, Dagobert D. and Schrickel, Harry G., *Encyclopedia of the Arts*, Philosophical Library, New York, 1946, p. 173.

Figure 68. MADONNA OF THE ROCKS by Leonardo da Vinci. In Florence, Leonardo da Vinci climaxes the use of chiaroscuro with strong atmospheric effects and a much bolder contrast of light and dark than his early Renaissance predecessors.

Courtesy Alinari-Art Reference Bureau, Louvre, Paris

Tenebrism

Painters who used violent chiaroscuro are called *tenebrists*. The first tenebrists were an international group of painters who, early in the seventeenth century, were inspired by the work of Michelangelo di Caravaggio. Caravaggio based his chiaroscuro on Correggio and instituted the so-called "dark-manner" of painting in Western Europe. Rembrandt became the technical adapter and perfector of this "dark-manner" which came to him through migratory artists of Germany and Southern Holland. The "dark-manner" made value an instrument in the characteristic exaggeration of baroque painting.

The strong contrasts lent themselves well to highly dramatic, even theatrical, work of this type. Later the dark-manner evolved into a pallid, muddy monotone which pervaded much of the nineteenth-century Western painting. The tenebrists and their followers were very much interested in peculiarities of lighting, particularly as it lent itself to *mood* or *emotional expression*. They deviated from *standard light conditions* by placing the implied light sources in *unexpected locations* creating unusual visual and spatial effects. In the hands of superior artists, such as Rembrandt, these effects were creative tools; in lesser hands, they became captivating tricks or visual sleight-of-hand.

Colorplate 25

Colorplate 26

Figure 69. ST. JOHN THE BAPTIST by Michelangelo da Caravaggio. He was essentially the leader in establishing the "dark-manner" of painting in the 16th and 17th centuries. Several of the North Italian painters before his time, however, such as Correggio, Titian and Tintoretto, show evidences of the tendency towards darker value composition.

Courtesy Nelson Fund, William Rockhill Nelson Gallery of Art, Atkins Museum of Fine Arts, Kansas City, Missouri.

Open and Closed Compositions

It is easy to see the emotive possibilities of value schemes, particularly as they relate to "closed" or "open" composition. Closed designs are those in which values are limited by *the edges* of *shapes* and *forms*. In open value composition the value areas may originate and end *as the artist sees fit*, sometimes conforming to the subject shapes, at times working independently of them, and, on occasion, doing both. The artist may employ closely related values for hazy, fog-like effects; or, he may use dramatically contrasting values creating sharply crystallized shapes. Thus value may run the gamut from decoration to violent expression.

Figure 70. READING (LA LECTURE) by Pablo Picasso. The values in this work are used in an "open" manner; the white value moves in and out of the figure in an arbitrary way, producing a shape not suggested by the original contours.

Courtesy The Museum of Modern Art, New York. Gift of Abby Aldrich Rockefeller.

DECORATIVE VALUE PATTERNS

Art styles which stress *decorative effects* usually ignore the conventional light source or neglect the representation of light altogether. If light effects appear, it is often in composite, *a selection of appearances* based on their contribution to the *total form* of the work. This admixture is characteristic of the art works of primitive and prehistoric tribes, children, traditional East Asians, and certain periods of Western art, notably the Middle Ages. Many contemporary art works are *completely free* of illusionistic lighting. Art work which thus divorces itself from *natural law* is obviously based on *pictorial invention, imagination,* and *formal considerations*. It is not by any means an art necessarily divorced from emotional impact (as witness, medieval art), but *the emotion* speaks primarily through the *forms,* and is consequently less extroverted.

The trend away from illumination values gained its strength in the nineteenth century partly as a result of the interest in art forms of the Near and Far East. This was given a Western *scientific interpretation* when Edouard Manet, a realist, observed that a multiplicity of light sources tended to *flatten object surfaces*. He found that this light condition would neu-

Figure 71. PRINCE RIDING AN ELEPHANT, Mughal: Period of Akbar. Signed: work of Khemkaran. Oriental artists often disregard the use of light (illumination) in favor of decorative value compositions.

Courtesy The Metropolitan Museum of Art, New York. Rogers Fund, 1925.

tralize *the plastic qualities* of objects, thus mini-mizing *gradations of value*. As a result, he laid his colors on canvas in *flat areas*, beginning with bright, light colors, and generally neglecting *shadow*. Some critics have claimed this to be the basic technical advance of the nineteenth century because it paved the way for *nonrep-resentational* uses of value and aided in the revival of interest in the shallow space concept.

Colorplate 27

Figure 73.

The photograph above demonstrates how light from one source emphasizes the three-dimensional qualities of the object and gives an indication of depth. This can be par-ticularly observed in the sculptured torso. The photograph below shows the same group of objects under the illumi-nation of several light sources. This form of lighting tends to flatten object surfaces and produces a more decorative effect.

Figure 72. NUIT DE NOEL by Henri Matisse. Matisse here uses values to produce a two-dimensional pattern instead of traditional chiaroscuro.

Courtesy The Museum of Modern Art, New York. Gift of Time, Inc., New York, New York.

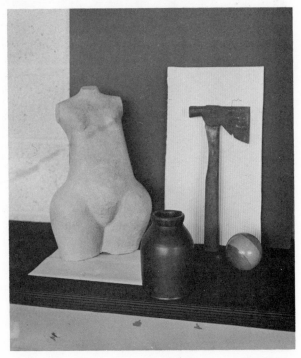

Figure 74.

Colorplate
28

COMPOSITIONAL FUNCTIONS OF VALUE

The idea of carefully controlled *shallow space* finds excellent illustration in the works of the early *cubists,* Picasso and Braque. In those paintings, space is given its order by the arrangement of *flat planes* abstracted from subject material. At first, the planes were shaded individually and semi-illusionistically, although there is no indication of any one light source. Later, *each plane* took on a *characteristic value* and, in combination with others, produced a carefully conceived *two-dimensional light-dark pattern.* Eventually the shallow spatial effect was developed in terms of *three-dimensional* pattern (or balance) through attention to the *advancing* and *receding* characteristics of value. The explorations of these artists in the early twentieth century helped to focus attention on the intrinsic significance of each and every element. Value was no longer forced to serve a *primary role* as a tool of *superficial transcription,* although it continued to be of descriptive usefulness. Most creative artists today think of value as a vital and organic participant in *pictorial organization,* affecting *dominance,* creating *two-dimensional pattern,* establishing *mood,* and producing *spatial unity.* It is a multi-purpose tool, and the success of the total work of art is, in large measure, based on the effectiveness with which the artist has made value serve these many functions.

Figure 75. MA JOLIE (WOMAN WITH A ZITHER OR GUITAR) by Pablo Picasso. The cubist, Picasso, in his explorations of the shallow space concept broke up natural forms into flat planes that are individually shaded and semi-illusionistically rendered.

Courtesy The Museum of Modern Art, New York. Acquired through the Lillie P. Bliss bequest.

VALUE PROBLEMS

PROBLEM 1

Different mediums have varying flexibilities in terms of their ability to create tones or values. The average person can easily discern about nine steps of value from white to black, but every medium varies in its ability to create these nine steps.

In areas about one inch square, create value scales from the lightest tone to the darkest tone possible. Try to create an individual scale for each of the following mediums: pencil, black crayon, pen and ink, dry-brush and ink, tempera paint varied with white and black, and water color modified by thinning the color.

Figure 76.

PROBLEM 2

The descriptive qualities of object surfaces are best defined by the value patterns created by light normally coming from above and originating from one source. These descriptive qualities may be enhanced and made more expressive by emphasizing the contrasts of light and dark where the edges of forms come together.

Select a group of simple still-life forms. Place a strong light above this still-life group directed either from the right or the left. Using any medium, create a picture using the natural group as a model. Copy the light and shadow patterns but feel free to exaggerate the tonal contrasts where forms overlap and where they meet the background.

PROBLEM 3

Value differences are of paramount importance when a student is investigating nature in objective drawing. Images in the natural world are perceived by the human eye mainly through the value contrasts of object surfaces.

With any suitable medium do a descriptive rendering from a still-life, a landscape, or a human figure. Begin by first observing the lightest and the darkest areas in the subject chosen; using these areas as a high and low measuring reference, relate all of the other values to them. Try to reproduce all details as accurately as possible.

Figure 77.

Problem 4

A multiplicity of contradictory light sources will flatten object surfaces. Such light will take away from the object its solid qualities, minimizing transitions of value gradation.

Using the same still-life group as in the preceding problem, change the direction and type of lighting. Using two or more strong lights, place them so that the light is from above and from both the right and left sides. (A light from in front would also increase the desired effect.) Using values created by mixing black and white tempera, copy the characteristic value patterns created by the objects in this group. Ignore any cast shadows which may result from one object being placed in front of another.

Problem 5

When values are considered only in terms of the shapes which they create, it is possible for more than one light-and-dark scheme to be effective. Individual artists often favor predominate dark values or predominate light values in their pictures. In fact, the expressive quality of a composition may vary depending upon whether the values are closely related or highly contrasting in character.

Invent a simple still-life arrangement using familiar forms such as fruit or vegetables. Keep the picture small so that it does not require too much time to paint the surfaces. Using black and white tempera or shading with pencil, create three different light-and-dark schemes for this composition. Do one which is composed of closely related light values; make the second of closely related dark values; and, finish the third by emphasizing highly contrasting values.

Figure 78.

Figure 79.

Problem 6

Most well-organized pictorial compositions have a definite dark-light pattern although they may exhibit a considerable range of values.

Using a color reproduction of a good painting as a model, try to represent its basic value pattern in terms of two tones, black and white. You will notice that there is usually a main large dark shape and a main large light shape.

Using the same picture for a model, develop its pattern in terms of three value tones, black, white, and a medium grey. You will notice that the medium tones serve as a transition between the contrasts of black and white. See if the greatest contrast of light and dark comes on the major shapes. (In doing this problem, forms do not have to be drawn in great detail but may be considerably simplified in character.)

PROBLEM 7

Value may create movement. The eye tends to follow a graded tone in much the same way as it follows a line. Thus graded tones are useful in creating a sense of unity by this tendency of the eye to follow a gradation.

Arrange a series of overlapping planes or volumes and increase the spatial movement into depth by grading the tones from light to dark or dark to light. Each plane may vary in order to create a gradation, or the gradation of value may take place on each individual shape to create movement.

Figure 80.

PROBLEM 8

Areas of value do not necessarily have to be rigidly restricted within the outlines of shapes. A given area of tone may belong to two different shapes, creating a greater unity of organization. An area of value does not have to be confined to an object border but may be opened and combined with other shapes.

Draw in line a group of still-life objects. Apply areas of varied darks, lights and textures which disregard the object contours. Overlap two or more objects and overlap the objects with the background in order to unify the overall picture.

Figure 81.

PROBLEM 9

A repetition of similar values in different parts of a pattern may create eye movements which unify the arrangement. Certainly the distribution of the proper sizes of value tones creates a controlled tension stabilizing a pictorial organization.

Fill a pictorial space with an arrangement of rectangles of varying size. These shapes may be separate, touching, or even overlapping, but a certain amount of empty or background space should be left around the forms. Create a medium value in the background space by using a series of parallel lines placed close together and in either a horizontal or a vertical relationship. Now fill in some of the rectangular shapes with solid black color and leave others white. See if you cannot create some paths of movement through the repetition of these dark values, at the same time distributing them so that a balanced effect will result. Variations in the sizes of similar value shapes will keep the effect from becoming monotonous. (Where two shapes of dark tone touch each other a white line may be left to separate the forms.)

This problem may be followed with one which uses rectangular volumes in space such as cubes or pyramids. When these solid forms are used, the values may be used on one, or two sides; however, the tones should be planned for the rhythm and balance they create, rather than a mere descriptive effect of light and shade.

PROBLEM 10

Just as with the other elements, a value pattern may have intrinsic meaning or support the emotional character of a mood. Psychologically, we often feel depressed when we note large areas of black, and man has tended to associate it with death, tragedy or despair. White usually makes us feel buoyant and open, or perhaps radiant.

To explore some of the moods or meanings that may be expressed with values, create a pictorial composition incorporating some of the ideas brought to mind by the list of titles which follows: Tempest, Tragedy, Hunger, Riot, Lost, Peace, Strikers, Ballet, Jazz Concert, Carnival. This may be done in a representational style, or more abstract shapes may be employed if desired.

Figure 82.

CHAPTER 7: TEXTURE

Definitions:

Tactile: A quality which refers to the sense of touch.

Texture: The actual or the illusion of tactile value on the surface of an area as created by nature or by man through his manipulation of the visual elements.

Actual Texture: A surface which stimulates a tactile response when actually touched.

Papier Collé: A technique of visual expression in which scraps of paper having various textures are actually pasted to the picture surface to enrich or embellish areas.

Collage: A similar technique to papiér collé but using a great variety of materials having tactile quality, not just paper alone.

Genre: Painting expressing subject matter which concerns everyday life, domestic scenes, sentimental family relationships, etc.

Illusionism: The imitation of visual reality created on the flat surface of the picture plane by the use of perspective, light-and-dark shading, etc.

Trompe l'oeil: A painting technique involving the copying of nature with such exactitude that the painted objects may be mistaken for the actual forms depicted.

Artificial Texture: Any texture created by man-made invention.

Natural Texture: Textures in actual objects which are created as the result of natural processes.

Invented Texture: Two-dimensional patterns created by the repetition of lines or shapes on a small scale over the surface of an area. The repeated motifs may be adaptation or borrowing of nature patterns used in a more regular or planned fashion.

Paint Quality: The use of the medium on surfaces to give them an enrichment through textural interest. Interest is created by the ingenuity in the handling of paint for its intrinsic character.

RELATIONSHIP OF TEXTURE TO THE VISUAL ARTS

Texture is unique among the art elements in that it activates two sensory processes at the same time. In viewing a picture the observer may recognize objects through the artist's depiction of characteristic *shape, color* and *value pattern*; he may also react to the surface character which the artist reminds him is typical of the object. Hence, there may be vivid feelings of touch, vicariously experienced, and complementing the sensations of vision.

Tactile response is the concern of the artist whether he is working in the *plastic* or the *graphic* field. The sculptor becomes involved with the problem of texture through his choice of media and the type and degree of finish to be given them. It is possible for him to recreate such textures as are characteristic of the subject if he feels so motivated. By cutting into the surface of the materials he can suggest the tactile qualities of hair, cloth, skin, or other textures which suit his purpose.

The graphic arts do not exist in the round, and any exaggerated attempt to fool the eye into believing this usually develops into a tour de force or violation of the medium. Although his opportunities to create texture are somewhat more limited than the sculptor's, the graphic artist nevertheless still has a formidable array of textural effects available to him. The items in our physical environment on which these are based may be *natural* (grass, leaves, stone, tree-bark, sand, etc.), or *artificial*, that is those created by man (paper, metal, glass, concrete, stucco, etc.).

TYPES OF TEXTURE
Actual

Colorplate
29
If the artist chooses to attach real materials to his work he is employing *actual texture*, one which can really be sensed through touch. The

category of actual texture may even include the medium with which he works, as it is applied to the working surface. Vincent van Gogh's paintings serve as a particularly good example of the surface qualities of medium. In Van Gogh's paintings rough textures have been produced by building up pigment on the canvas. It is significant that painters such as Van Gogh regard actual textures of any kind as an aid to *academic illusionism*, as well as expression. Texture is usually pasted or painted according to the varied needs of the design rather than as a strict description of the properties of particular objects. In many cases the texture of the canvas is left bare as a reminder that it is part of a flat *painting*, not a *literal* slice of nature.

Figure 83. HEAD OF CHRIST by William Zorach. Zorach has polished portions of the surface of the head of Christ in order to bring out the natural textural quality of granite. He has roughened selected surfaces which seem suitable for the stimulation of subject characteristics.

Courtesy The Museum of Modern Art, New York. Mrs. John D. Rockefeller, Jr. Fund.

papier collé

A growing appreciation of texture as an integral part of form led to many textural experiments early in the twentieth century. The *cubists* were very much involved in this experimentation. Their explorations of pictorial functions of texture led to an art form known as *papier collé,* a technique involving the pasting of bits of newspaper, stamps, tickets, etc. directly on the picture surface. The printed and cut or torn passages of these pieces created patterns which enlivened selected areas.

collages

Eventually this use of paper was broadened to include the use of wire, wood, sandpaper, in fact any and all surfaces whose textures were appropriate and usable in the paintings. Compositions made up of scraps of this kind are called *collages.* The picture may be nothing but material arrangements (at times based on subject material, at other times nonrepresentational), or these may be combined with drawn and painted passages.

Actual texture shows some very inventive exploitation in the works of contemporary artists. Aggregates, such as sand, are sometimes mixed with paint to provide a textured medium. Material surfaces of different textural properties are occasionally substituted for the conventional canvas. Furrows and ridges in the paint, of various textural patterns, are produced through the use of appropriate and convenient tools of any source and description. Textures are also transferred from materials by pressing them against the wet paint. Works are further enriched by combinations of media within them, some chalky, oily, coarse, smooth, heavy, thin, etc. The ethic of such practices is now limited only by the ability of the artist to use them to produce an integrated and harmonious effect.

Figure 84. The student work reproduced below is an example of "papier collé" meaning that paper shapes have been cut and pasted down to form a picture. The paper used has been selected according to the decorative interest provided by its textures. The interest is further enhanced by the fact that the textures do not always correspond to the characteristic surfaces of objects depicted.

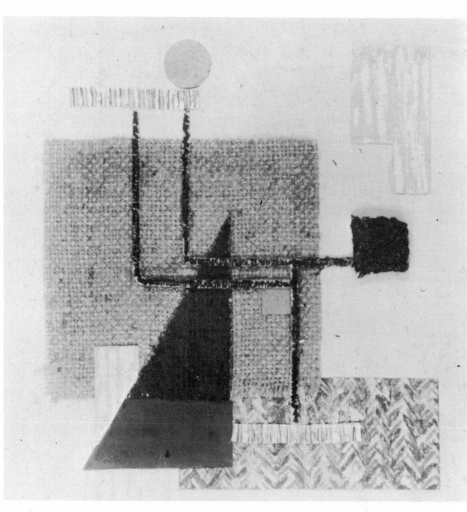

Figure 85. Collages are created out of any actual materials which have texture interest and can be fastened to a flat working surface. They may be used for the simulation of natural textures, but are usually created for decorative purposes.

Simulated Texture

Simulated textures are very common in the field of art. Such textures call for a careful rendering or copying of the light and dark patterns created by surface character. This is essentially an academic procedure but it may be given creative application. The Dutch and Flemish artists produced amazingly naturalistic effects in still-life and genre paintings. Their work shows the evident relish with which they moved from one texture detail to another. Simulated textures are often associated with *trompe l'oeil* paintings which make a blatant attempt to "fool the eye." These paintings usually pay little attention to the factors involved in formal organization but are of some interest as examples of an isolated technique.

Colorplate
30

Invented Texture

A third type of texture is one which may be called *invented*; at times, these textures may have their source in nature, but they undergo a very positive metamorphosis in the hands of the artist, who changes them according to the needs of his work. In this case, the texture may more properly be described as *decorative pattern* for it usually becomes two-dimensional in its effects. It is nonrepresentational, ordinarily geometric (although it may also be amorphous and biomorphic) and, having been created, is potentially of high aesthetic quality. Invented texture may develop out of the artist's programmatic search for a suitable embellishment through accident of technique or a mingling of media; the origin is really of little consequence if it functions effectively within the framework of the design.

Figure 86. GIRL BEFORE A MIRROR by Pablo Picasso. The stripes and patterns which form such a striking embellishment for this painting may originate in nature or in the artist's mind. They perform an essential function within the design in establishing decorative space, dominant areas, and rhythmic passage through the work. Such textures may be termed invented.

TEXTURE AND PATTERN

The differentiation between *pattern* and *texture* is often ignored or misunderstood and deserves some clarification. *Pattern* might be defined as a decorative design, involving some repetition of motif which may, or may not, have derived from some texture. Pattern is ordinarily regarded as being essentially *two-dimensional* or flat; it has no tactile pretensions. Texture, on the other hand, invariably creates pattern but also invokes a tactile response. A simulated texture is basically a pattern and is textural only to the degree that it reminds one of his sense of touch. An actual texture is of a dual nature, preeminently texture but also producing pattern. Invented textures may develop to the point at which textural suggestions are of no consequence; at this point, *descriptive* function is exceeded by *decorative* function. No exact line can be drawn between pattern and texture; the distinction would have to be made in terms of the particular area under consideration.

ORIGINS OF CONTEMPORARY TEXTURAL AWARENESS

The interest in texture is an obvious part of contemporary design. The revolutionary art concepts of the last seventy years spawned analyses of naked form and an appreciation for simple, even stark, areas. It was necessary to strip objects bare in order to expose and reevaluate the

Figure 87. FISHES by Amelia Pelaez del Casal. In this painting we find both texture and pattern. The areas on the fish are decorative in nature, but are derived from actual surface quality whereas other patterns in the painting simply add interest to areas and are essentially visual rather than tactile in their appeal. They may originate, however, with the pattern found in textures of the original subject.

Courtesy The Museum of Modern Art, New York. Inter-American Fund.

Colorplate 29. SELF-PORTRAIT by Vincent van Gogh. The massing of paint on van Gogh's canvases creates actual textures. The application of paint is often directly from the tube or "built-up" and scraped clean with the palette knife. The ribbons of paint in his work follow or create the rhythm sensed in nature and frequently simulate natural forms.

Colorplate 30. THE ANNUNCIATION by Jan van Eyck. Jan van Eyck's work is typically Flemish in that it shows the pleasure with which he selected and simulated textures in his paintings. He delighted in detailed explorations of contrasting materials.

Courtesy The National Gallery of Art, Washington, D.C. Andrew Mellon Collection.

Colorplate 31. HIDE-AND-SEEK by Pavel Tchelitchew. The use of a personal, textural style is greatly responsible for much of the emotional quality present in this painting. Here, instead of the obvious invented patterns, we find the subtle textural treatment of organic matter which evokes a feeling of biological mystery.

Collection The Museum of Modern Art, New York. Mrs. Simon Guggenheim Fund.

underlying structure in terms of pictorial form. This reevaluation is historically complete, and the emphasis on basic form is generally considered desirable; but we now find many evidences of a hunger for the adornment of the naked members of pictorial structure. This desire has been aided and abetted by the revelations of the sharp and penetrating focus of the microscope and camera. The urge to decorate is amply revealed by an inspection of the professionally designed products and types of home furnishings now being offered. Everywhere the use of texture is in evidence; on our walls, and floors, in our fabrics, on everything we use and value in our daily living. Most of this is the direct result of the evolution of contemporary art styles, and it continues to exist in those styles through the artist's use of actual, simulated, and invented textures.

FORMAL FUNCTIONS OF TEXTURE

In terms of pictorial function the use of texture has certain perils as well as advantages. Texture contributes greatly to the richness and visual pleasure afforded by a work of art, but only if it is kept within the bounds of judicious restraint. Overuse of texture may place a false emphasis on that element destroying the unity of the work as a whole. Carelessly employed, it may disrupt the coherence of pattern by isolating areas; it can also produce spatial discontinuity, i.e., the texture may detach itself from the surface on which it is presumed to exist. Properly used, however, texture becomes an integral part of the value and color plan of the art work.

Emotional Properties of Texture

Texture has the property of enhancing *emotional expression*. By the magnifying of texture or placing it in unlikely locations, the artist can make the desired effect much more vivid, or even shocking, if need be. Certain types of textures are generally associated with certain environments, experiences, or objects which in themselves may become symbolic. When we say that a man is as "slippery as a snake," we are

equating tactile sensations with attributes of character. Texture in contexts such as this may be utilized as a supplementary psychological device.

Spatial Properties of Texture

Spatially, finely detailed texture denotes nearness, and conversely, blurred or indistinct detail suggests distance. The degree or type of texture of a unit depends on the observer's physical reference. For example, a leaf surface will differ in appearance depending on whether it is seen through a microscope, at arm's length, or from a considerable distance where its association with other leaves may produce a new, and bushy, texture. In *academic painting*, the use of texture is always typical of a given spatial situation, but an artist with more creative intentions may take his texture effects from near and far, using them together to achieve *controlled* space variations, or to create arresting contradictions.

Two-Dimensional Uses of Texture

The use of texture for a *spatial purpose* immediately sets up the requirement that the same texture function effectively in a *two-dimensional* sense as well. The great power of attraction exerted by texture makes it a useful tool in controlling the *relative dominance of the subject material*; the spotting of textures throughout the pictorial area will always affect the existing pattern for good or ill. Texture contrast must be magnified or minimized according to this consideration. An existing shape may tend to dominate the entire picture if it is given an exciting texture. On the other hand, a negligible area, if highly textured, might successfully contend with the larger shape for the observer's attention. Every successful work of art makes each element serve as many roles as possible.

In summary, texture is seen as being useful in description of object, stimulation of tactile responses, enrichment of pictorial areas, clarification of spatial suggestions, and control of pattern in terms of relative dominance.

Colorplate
31

TEXTURE PROBLEMS

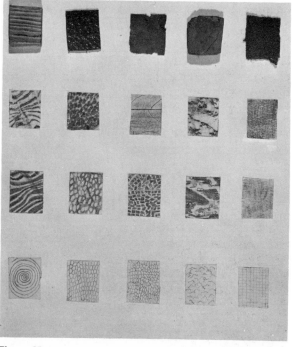

PROBLEM 1

Textures can be actual, simulated, invented, or abstracted.

Select four contrasting, flat, actual textures. Using these actual textures as models, create four simulated textures. Using the actual textures over again as guides, create four abstract textures. In addition, create four invented textures. Mount all of the textures on a cardboard background placing the four actual textures at the top. Group the remaining textures under their actual texture models.

Figure 88.

PROBLEM 2

Each medium used by the artist is capable of creating its own distinctive textures. The artist, in order to be expressive, must understand the varying flexibilities of the different media which may be used.

Divide a large sheet of drawing paper into a number of rectangular areas. Create a design pattern over the whole area of the paper. Finish by changing mediums and style of handling the medium in each rectangular area; for example, drawing ink may be used with fine pen lines in one area and with brush lines in another area. (The example illustrated shows areas of pencil, crayon, ink, water color, and tempera paint.)

Figure 89.

PROBLEM 3

Texture rubbings can quickly guide a student to the infinite varieties of actual and simulated textures.

Place a piece of white paper over a coarse textured surface. Rub over the paper with a soft pencil or crayon. The rubbing technique will bring out a negative impression of the textured surface. Repeat the procedure on a variety of surfaces. Assemble these textures in a chart or a pictorial organization.

PROBLEM 4

The different mediums employed by the artist automatically result in varying surface effects which enhance the character of the shapes used. These changes of textural character may take the place of the interest created by varying shape styles. Frequently, texture variation has become a form of decoration.

Using a wide variety of mediums, experiment with their manipulation to see how many different types of surface can be created. Use both point and side of the pencil varying pressure strokes together for diverse effects. Try mixing mediums such as ink over crayon strokes, water color wash over crayon tones, shading with pencil strokes over color washes, penlines drawn in wet water color washes, brush strokes of tempera paint in wet washes of transparent water color, etc.

These effects should be applied to areas from one inch to four inches in size. Cut simple shapes such as squares, rectangles, or triangles from these areas and assemble in a simple, decorative shape organization; try using one kind of shape only but varying the sizes. These shapes may touch, overlap, or be completely separate, but the organization should be simple in character. In other words, we should depend on the texture variation for interest, not the complexity of the design relationships. Remember to leave a number of areas of plain background around many of the shapes, because too much texture variation can become chaotic.

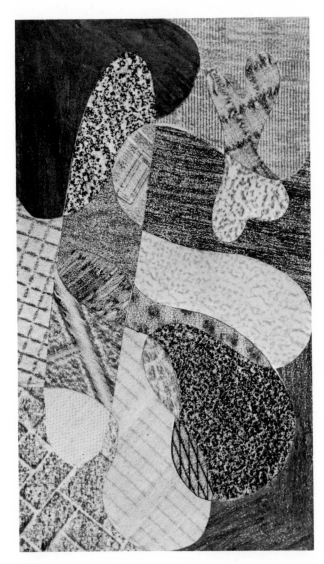

Figure 90.

Figure 91.

PROBLEM 5

The graphic artist is often deeply interested in making his visual surfaces more varied and exciting. When he is primarily concerned with presenting his picture as a tangible object and not as an illusion of nature, he may use *actual* textures. In creating such an artistic form the artist may add unusual materials to the surface such as gluing papers of varying patterns, colors, and textures. When bits of paper are pasted together on a picture surface, it is termed a *papier collé*.

Gather several varieties of paper (i.e. newspaper, construction paper, cellophane, tinfoil, printed color sheets, etc.). Cut, tear, paste, and assemble this paper on a flat surface so that it will have an expressive, as well as sound structural form.

Figure 92.

PROBLEM 6

One medium used with ingenuity by the artist can create considerable texture variation.

On a plain piece of white drawing paper scribble with light pencil a continuous line movement. Try to vary the line as it moves all around and through the space crossing and recrossing itself until it returns to the starting point. Do not worry about the pattern becoming too complex because all small, separate shapes do not have to be seen individually but may be combined to create larger shapes. Create a pattern by filling in many of the shapes created with decorative textures made with colored crayon line, dots, small shapes, etc. Fill in many of the areas with solid crayon so that some of the textures are separated by plain areas. Areas of color which touch each other should be distinctly contrasting in color, value, or character. This pattern could be unified by using a heavy black line around all the shapes or applying a wash of dark color over all the crayon lines.

Figure 93.

PROBLEM 7

In addition to merely using paper for actual textures, as in papier collé, the artist may add other foreign materials to the picture surface. Among these may be such items as string, wire, cotton, cork, rubber, plastic, sponge, sticks, pipe cleaners, sand, gravel, soap, buttons, pebbles, candy, etc. When many such materials are glued to the picture surface, it is called a *collage*.

Gather several varieties of textured materials such as those listed in the preceding paragraph. Cut, paste, and assemble these materials together on a picture surface into an expressive arrangement. Also use passages of normal media such as paint, chalk, crayon, pencil, or ink.

Figure 94.

PROBLEM 8

The interest in pictures or designs made of mosaic tile is largely due to the effects created by putting small colored pieces together. The effect of mosaic may be simulated by using small pieces of colored paper.

Create an abstract design or picture by using small pieces of colored paper cut from magazine illustrations and fitted together to form shapes. An interesting effect can be obtained if some of the colors used already have slight texture variations. To keep the design from becoming *too* confusing certain precautions are necessary; do not use too small nor too complex shapes and make sure that the colors chosen for different shapes are definitely contrasting in value.

Figure 95.

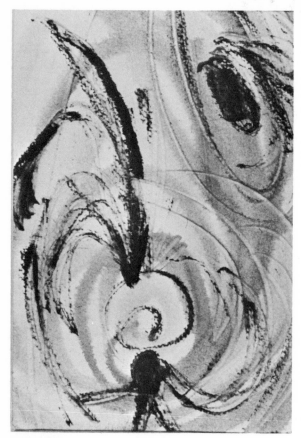

Figure 96.

PROBLEM 9

The effects of texture in a flexible medium such as water color are frequently accidental and are especially entrancing because of this unexpected quality.

Experiment with water color minglings by placing areas of color together while wet and allow one to flow into the other. This flow can be effected by tipping the paper or by blowing the wet color in various directions. If the paper is dampened before color is applied, a still different type of texture results. Sometimes a resemblance to natural shapes is seen in a water color mingling; this shape could be further defined by a pen-and-ink or brush line made while the surface is damp or after it has dried. The result then might be a pictorial representation of natural forms but with unusual and unexpected textural quality.

Figure 97.

PROBLEM 10

Other variations on accidental textures employed by the artist may be arrived at by treating the surface in a variety of ways before applying any medium.

Employing a piece of strong, white paper, break up the picture field into varying sized areas and explore the possibilities of varying the surface texture of the paper by needling, scoring, scraping, crumbling, rubbing, folding, and sanding.

Media may then be added to the picture surface and treated in like manner.

CHAPTER 8: COLOR

Definitions:

Color: The character of a surface which is the result of the response of vision to the wavelength of light reflected from that surface.

Spectrum: The band of individual colors which results when a beam of light is broken up into its component hues.

Pigments: Any material or medium used by the artist to create the effect of color on a surface.

Neutrals: Surface tones which do not reflect any single wavelength of light but rather all of them at once. No single color is then noticed but only a sense of light or dark such as white, grey, or black.

Hue: This designates the common name of a color and indicates its position in the spectrum or in the color circle. Hue is determined by the specific wavelength of the color in the ray of light.

Value: The characteristic of a color in terms of the amount of light reflected from it. It refers to the lightness or darkness of tone, not to its color *quality*.

Intensity: The saturation or strength of a color determined by the *quality* of light reflected from it. A vivid color is of high intensity, a dull color of low intensity.

Neutralized Color: A color which has been "greyed" or reduced in intensity by mixture with any of the neutrals or with a complementary color.

Objective Color: The naturalistic color of an object as seen by the eye (green grass, blue sky, red fire, etc.).

Subjective Color: Colors chosen by the artist without regard to the natural appearance of the object portrayed. They have nothing to do with objective reality but represent the expression of the individual artist.

Analogous Colors: Those colors which are closely related in hue. They are usually adjacent to each other on the color wheel.

Color Triad: A group of three colors spaced an equal distance apart on the color wheel. There is a primary triad, a secondary triad, and two intermediate triads on the twelve-color wheel.

Complementary Colors: Two colors which are directly opposite each other on the color wheel. A primary color would be complementary to a secondary color which was a mixture of the two remaining primaries.

Color Tonality: An orderly planning in terms of selection and arrangement of color schemes or color combinations. It would concern itself not only with hue, but also with value and intensity relationships.

NATURE OF COLOR

Color is the element of *form* which arouses the most universal appreciation and the one to which we are the most sensitive. It has an instant appeal to the child as well as to the adult; even an infant will be attracted by a *brightly colored* object more than by one which is *dull* in appearance. The average layman, who is frequently puzzled by what he calls "modern" art, usually finds its color exciting and attractive. He may question the use of distortions of shape but seldom objects to the use of *color*, providing that it is harmonious in character; in fact, he frequently likes a work for its color style alone.

Color is one of the most expressive elements, because its quality affects our emotions *directly* and *immediately*. The average viewer of a work of art does not have to rationalize what he is *supposed to feel* about color, but has an immediate *emotional* reaction to it. Pleasing rhythms and harmonies of color satisfy our *aesthetic* desires. We "like" certain combinations of color and reject others. In representational art, color serves to identify objects and to create the effect of illusionistic space. Color differs from the other elements in that it deals with certain scientific facts and principles which are exact and may easily be systematized. The general approach in this chapter will be to examine the basic facts or characteristics of *color relationships,* and then to see how they function in giving *form* and *meaning* to the *subject matter* of the artist's work.

Source of Color

Color begins with and is derived from *light,* either natural or artificial. Where there is little *light,* there is little *color;* where the light is strong, the color is apt to be particularly intense in character. We notice at such times of day as dusk or dawn, when the light is weak, that it is difficult to distinguish one color from another. Under bright, strong sunlight, such as we find in tropic climates, colors seem to take on an additional intensity. Every ray of light coming from the sun is composed of different *waves* which vibrate at different speeds. The *sensation of color* is aroused in the human mind by the way our sense of vision responds to the different *wavelengths* of light which affect it. This fact can be experimentally proven by allowing a beam of light to pass through a triangularly shaped piece of glass (prism) and then reflect-

Figure 98.

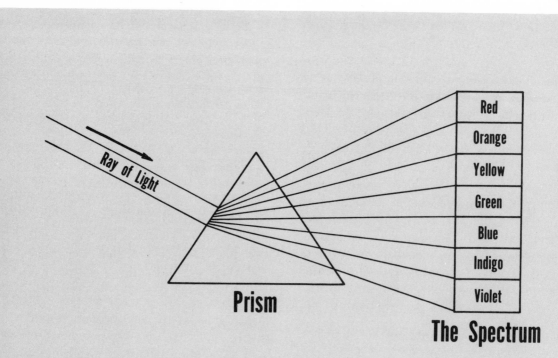

ed from a sheet of white paper. The rays of light are bent or refracted as they pass through the glass at different angles (according to their wavelength) and are reflected from the white paper as different *colors*. Our sense of vision then interprets these colors as individual stripes in a narrow band which we call *the spectrum*. The major colors easily distinguishable in this band are red, orange, yellow, green, blue, indigo, and violet. (The scientist uses the term, *indigo*, for the color which the artist usually calls *blue-violet*.) These colors, however, blend together gradually so that we can see several intermediate colors between them.

The colors of the spectrum are, of course, pure and represent the greatest *intensity* (brightness) possible. If we could collect all of these *spectrum colors* and mix them in a reverse process, we would again have white light. The *pigments* or coloring matter which the artist uses are not as strong in intensity nor as pure as the *spectrum colors*. In working with pigments, all of the colors mixed will not produce *white*, but rather a *grey* which, in a sense, is an *impure or darkened* form of white.

Since all of the colors are present in a beam of light, how then are we able to distinguish *one color* as it is reflected from a natural object? Any colored object has certain physical properties called color quality or *pigmentation* which enable it to *absorb* some of the color waves and *reflect* others. A green leaf will appear green to the eye because it reflects the green waves in the ray of light while absorbing all the other colors. A *pigment,* such as the artist uses, is a substance which has this property, and, when applied to the surface of an object, gives it the same property. A basic fact to remember is that color in art, depending on *pigments,* can only approximate the intensity of the *spectrum colors* of light. Hereafter in discussing *color,* the word will be taken to refer to the artist's *pigment* rather than the sensation of *colored light.*

Neutrals

All objects, of course, do not have this quality of color. Some are black, white, or grey which do not look like any of the colors of the spec-

trum. No *color quality* is found in them but they merely differ in the *quantity of light* which is reflected from them. Because we do not distinguish any *one* color, these tones are called *neutrals.* From the standpoint of the scientists, these neutrals actually reflect *all* of the color waves in a ray of light. One neutral, absolute black, (seldom seen) reflects no light at all and consequently has no color. White may be called the total *addition* of color, because it is the result of a surface reflecting all of the color waves in light to an *equal degree.* Black then is usually called the *absence* of color, because it results when a surface absorbs all of the color rays *equally* and reflects *none* of them. If white represents a one hundred per cent reflection of light, then any grey may be considered an impure white because it is created by only a *partial* reflection of all of the color waves in the spectrum. If the quantity of light reflected is great, the grey is light in value; if the amount reflected is little, the grey is dark in tone. The neutrals are affected by the *quantity of light* reflected, whereas color is concerned with the *quality of light* reflected.

Physical Properties of Color

As previously mentioned, we find in the spectrum such colors as red, orange, yellow, blue, green, and violet. These are only a few colors and yet we know that hundreds of *color variations* exist. The child or the beginning worker with color is likely to use only a few simple, pure colors of the spectrum. He does not seem to realize that the simple spectrum colors can be varied in three specific ways. Every color of the spectrum actually exists in *many* forms although these forms may continue to bear the simple *spectrum name*. There are *many reds* for example which differ in character from the *pure red* which we find in the spectrum. Every color which the artist uses must be described in terms of three physical properties, *Hue, Value,* and *Intensity.*

hue

This is the property or characteristic of a color which refers to its *position* in the spectrum. It may also be said to refer to the *color*

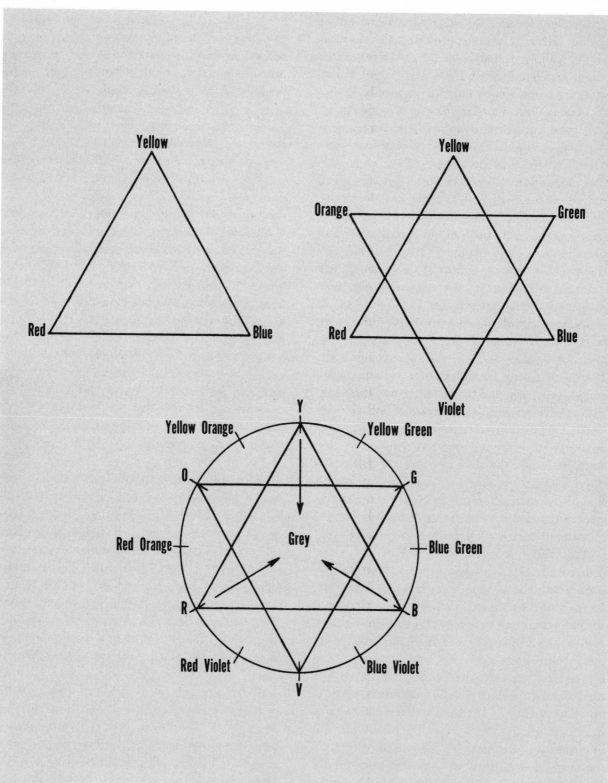

Figure 99. This diagram indicates: first, the primary triad; second, the addition of the three secondary colors; and third, the placement of the six immediate colors. In theory, the three primary colors when mixed will neutralize each other and produce off grey.

name which is used to differentiate the colors having different wavelengths of light. For example, yellow is one hue which differs from green, another hue, and has a different wavelength. A color may change its hue only by being mixed with another *color* in the spectrum; this makes an actual change in the wavelength of the ray of light. The same yellow, if added to green, creates a yellowish green or a change in hue. Also yellow mixed with blue creates green and the amount of yellow used will determine the kind of green which results. Yellow, yellow green, green, and blue green are all different hues because they change in their wavelength. However, in mixing them with *pigments*, each contains the *common hue,* yellow; such variations are called *analagous hues.*

Many colors of the spectrum may be created by mixing two other colors, such as orange from red and yellow, or violet from red and blue. There are three colors, however, which cannot be created from mixtures; these are the hues, red, yellow, and blue. They are called the *primary* colors. When these three primaries are mixed in pairs, or all together in equal or unequal amounts, they can produce all of the possible colors. A mixture of the three primaries should theoretically result in white; actually this mixture produces a neutral *grey* which may be considered a darkened form of white. The important thing to remember is that the three primaries *neutralize* each other so that the resulting tone does not resemble *any one hue.* By mixing any two primaries we arrive at a *secondary* color, such as orange from red and yellow, or green from yellow and blue. In addition, there are certain *intermediate* colors created by the mixture of a primary with a neighboring secondary color. There is actually no limit to the number of intermediate colors because a change of proportion in the amount of primary or secondary colors used will make a change in the resultant hue. In other words, there is no one yellow green possible by mixing green and yellow; if more yellow is used it is a different yellow green from the one resulting when more green is used.

In order to systematize color relationships, the hues are usually represented as being arranged around a wheel. The three *primary* colors are spaced at equal distances apart on this circle with yellow usually placed at the top. The three *secondary* colors are then placed in between the primaries from which they are mixed. In between each primary and each secondary color an *intermediate* color is placed, the whole resulting in a twelve color circle. As we move around this color circle, there is a change in the *hue* of the colors, because there is an actual change in the wavelength of light rays which produce them. The closer together colors appear on this wheel, the closer their *hue relationships*; the farther apart any two hues are, the more contrasting they are in character. The hues which appear directly opposite each other afford the greatest contrast and are known as *complementary* colors.

value

In mixing colors, we discover that a wide range of color tones may be produced by using one *hue* and modifying it with the addition of the *neutrals,* black or white. This would indicate that colors have characteristics other than hue. The property of color known as *value* distinguishes between the lightness and darkness of colors, or the *quantity of light* which a color reflects. It is possible to have many *value* steps between the darkest and lightest appearance of *any one hue.* To change the tone value of a pigment, we must mix another pigment with it which is darker or lighter in character. The only dark or light pigments available which would not also change the hue of a color are black and white.

All of the colors of the spectrum reflect a different *quantity* of light as well as a different *wavelength.* A large amount of light is reflected from yellow whereas a small amount of light is reflected from violet. Each color, at its spectrum intensity, has a *normal value* which indicates the *amount of light* it reflects. It can, however, be made lighter or darker than normal by the addition of white or black as previously noted. It is important to know the normal value of each of the spectrum colors in order to use them most effectively. This *normal value* can be most easily seen when the colors of the wheel are placed in relationship to a scale of *neutral values* from black to white.

	White	
	High light	Yellow
Yellow orange	Light	Yellow green
Orange	Low light	Green
Red orange	Medium	Blue green
Red	High dark	Blue
Red violet	Dark	Blue violet
Violet	Low dark	
	Black	

This chart may be said to indicate the relative *normal values* of the hues at their *spectrum intensity* (purity or brilliance).

intensity

The third property of color, *intensity* (sometimes called saturation or chroma) refers to the *quality of light* in a color. In this way, it differs from value which refers to the *quantity of light* which a color reflects. We use the term *intensity* in distinguishing a brighter tone of a color from a duller one of the *same hue*; that is to say, a color which has a high degree of saturation or strength from one which is greyed or *neutralized* in character. The saturation point or the purest color is actually found in the spectrum produced by a beam of light passing through a prism. However, the pigment used by the artist which comes closest to resembling this color is said to be at *spectrum intensity*. The purity of the light waves reflected from the pigment produces the variation in the brightness or dullness of the color. For example, a pigment which reflected only the red rays of light would be an intense red; but if any of the complementary green rays were reflected also, the effect would be to dull or *neutralize* the brightness of the red color. If the green and red rays balance each other equally, the resulting tone would be a *neutral grey*; consequently, as a color loses its intensity, it tends to approach or resemble a grey.

There are actually four ways of changing the intensity of colors when mixing pigments. Three of these are accomplished by adding to the hue pigment a neutral that is black, white, or grey. As white is added to any hue, the resulting tone becomes lighter in *value* but it also loses its brightness or *intensity of color*. In the same way, when black is added to a hue, the *intensity* diminishes as the *value* darkens. In other words, we cannot change value *without* changing intensity although these two properties are not the *same*. When using the third method of changing *intensity,* a neutral grey of the *same value* is mixed with the *spectrum color*. The mixture then will be a variation in intensity *without* a change in value; the color will become less *bright* as more grey is added but will not get lighter or darker in tone. The fourth way of changing the intensity of any hue is by adding some of the complementary hue. As has been previously mentioned, the mixture of two hues which occur exactly opposite each other on the color wheel, such as red and green, blue and orange, or yellow and violet will result in a *neutral grey*. This is because the complementary colors represent an *equal balance* of the three *primaries*. The dominating hue in the mixture of two complementary colors will give its specific character to the resulting tone; consequently this tone, instead of being a pure grey, will be a greyed or neutralized form of the color which is used in *the larger amount*. When hues are neutralized by mixing complements, the resulting colors have a certain liveliness of character not present when they are neutralized with a *grey pigment*. This interesting character is further enhanced when the complementary tones are not actually mixed but are merely placed close together in little dots of broken color. The mixture then actually takes place in the visual sensation of the observer.

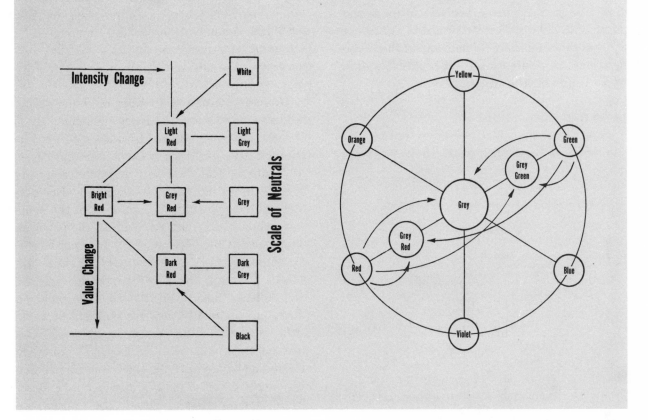

Figure 100. This diagram illustrates the four means of changing the intensity of color. (1) In the diagram on the left as white (a neutral) is added to bright red, the value is changed but the resulting color is lowered in intensity. (2) In the same way, the addition of black to bright red creates a dark red shown closer to the neutral scale because the intensity is changed. (3) When a neutral grey is added to the spectrum color, the intensity is lowered but the value is neither raised nor lowered. (4) The diagram on the right indicates a change of intensity by adding to a color a little of its complement. For instance, by adding a small amount of green to red a grey red is produced. In the same way a small amount of red added to green results in a grey green. When the two colors are balanced (not necessarily equal amounts) the resulting mixture is a neutral grey.

Color Relationships

The key to the successful use of color depends upon an understanding of *color relationships*. A single color, by itself, may have a certain character, but that character may be greatly changed when it is seen with other colors. Colors may be closely related or they may be contrasting, but the contrast can vary considerably in *degree*. The greatest contrast in hue occurs when two colors are used together which appear directly opposite each other on the color wheel. There is a shorter interval between colors and consequently less contrast

when *three* colors are used which are *spaced equally* distant apart on the color wheel. The first group, known as the primary triad, consists of red, yellow, and blue; the second group or secondary triad is composed of orange, green, and violet. The contrast is more striking in the *primary* triad; in the *secondary* triad, although the *interval* between hues is the same, the contrast is softer. This effect probably takes place because in any pair of the triad there is a *common color*; orange and green both contain yellow, orange and violet both contain red, and green and violet both contain blue. Where colors actually appear next to each other on the color wheel we have the shortest interval and consequently the closest relationship. Three or four *neighboring* hues (analogous colors) always contain *one common color* which dominates the group. (See diagram below.)

warm and cool colors

All of the colors which we know are usually thought of as belonging to one of two groups, the *warm colors* or the *cool colors*. Red, orange, and yellow colors usually associated with the sun or fire and are considered *warm*. Any colors containing blue, such as green, violet, or blue green are associated with air, sky, and water, and are called *cool colors*. This quality of warmth or coolness in a color may be affected or even changed by the hues *around* or *near* it. The artist may mix a color on his *palette* and then find it appears entirely different when

Figure 101.

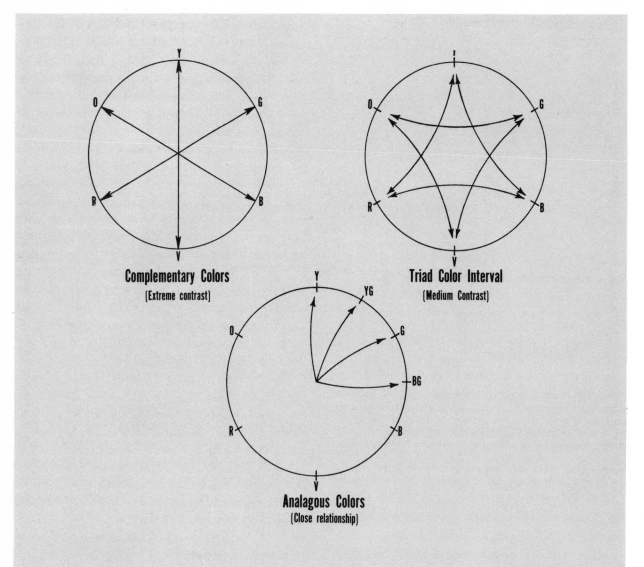

Complementary Colors
(Extreme contrast)

Triad Color Interval
(Medium Contrast)

Analagous Colors
(Close relationship)

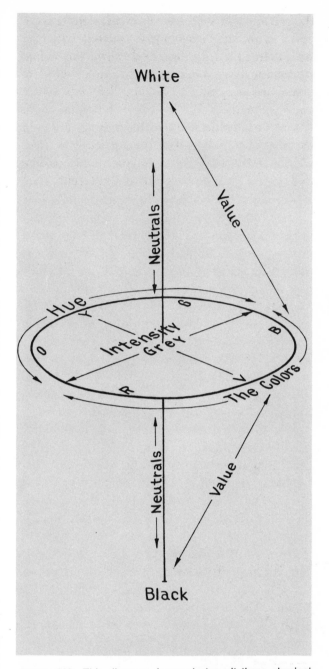

Figure 102. This diagram demonstrates all three physical properties of color. We can see all of the color variations as existing on a three-dimensional solid (a double cone). As the colors move around this solid, they change in hue. When these hues move upward or downward on the solid, they change in value. As all of the colors on the outside move toward the center, they become closer to the neutral values and there is a change in intensity.

it appears on the *canvas* in juxtaposition to other colors.

simultaneous contrast

Colorplate 32

The effect of one tone upon another is sometimes expressed as the RULE OF SIMULTANEOUS CONTRAST. According to this rule, whenever two different color tones come into direct contact, the contrast will intensify the *difference* between them. The effect is most noted, of course, when the colors are directly *contrasting* in hue, but it even occurs if the colors have some degree of *relationship*. For example, a yellow green surrounded by green will appear to be yellow, whereas if it were surrounded by yellow, it would be more noticeably green. The contrast used can be in the characteristics of *intensity or value* as well as in *hue*. A greyed blue will look *brighter* if placed against a grey background; it will look *greyer* or more neutralized against a bright blue background. The most obvious or strongest effect occurs when directly opposite or *complementary hues* are juxtaposed; blue is brightest when seen next to orange, and green is brightest when seen next to red. When a warm tone is seen in simultaneous contrast to a cool tone, the warm tone is warmer and the cool tone cooler. A color always tends to bring out its complement in a neighboring color. When a neutralized grey is placed next to a strong positive color, it tends to take on a *hue character* complementary to the positive color. When a person wears a certain color in clothing, it tends to emphasize or bring out the *opposite color* in his complexion.

All of these changes in color feeling should make us realize that no one color should be used for its character alone, but should be considered in relation to the other colors present. For this reason, it is better to develop a color composition *all at once* rather than trying to finish one area completely before going on to another. Only after gaining a knowledge of the basic facts of color and effects of color relationship can we go on to its function as an *element of form* in composition.

USES OF COLOR

Being familiar with the sources of color and its principal properties will be of little value to us unless we can understand how these facts are used by the artist to accomplish his purpose. Color serves several different purposes in artistic composition. It must be understood, however, that these purposes are not always separate and distinct but frequently overlap and are interrelated. Color may be used in the following ways:

1. To give spatial quality to the pictorial field.
   a. Color may supplement, or even substitute for, value differences in order to give plastic quality.
   b. Color may create interest through the counterbalance of backward and forward movement in pictorial space.
2. To create mood and symbolize ideas.
3. To serve as a vehicle for the expression of personal emotions and feelings.
4. To attract and direct attention as a means of giving organization to a composition.
5. To accomplish aesthetic appeal by a system of well-ordered color relationships.
6. To identify objects by describing the *superficial facts* of their *appearance*.

The last of these functions was considered of greatest importance when painting was looked upon as a purely *illustrational* art. For a long period in the history of Western art, color was looked upon as something which came from the object being represented. Color in painting used to indicate the natural appearance of an object is known as *local color*. A more expressive quality is likely to be achieved when the artist is willing to disassociate the color surfaces in the painting from the *object* to which the color supposedly belongs. In place of local color, an entirely *subjective* color treatment may be substituted; the colors used and their relationships become the *invention of the artist* for purposes other than mere representation. This style of treatment may even *deny* color as an *objective reality*; that is, we may have purple cows, green faces, or red trees. Most of the functions of color mentioned previously are largely *subjective in character*; they are of particular importance in contemporary art and should be examined separately.

Colorplates 33, 34 (margin note)

Plastic Quality of Color

As used by the present day artist, color which does not describe the surface of an object may be used to give the essential reality of its plastic character. This ability of color to *build a form* comes from the advancing and receding characteristics of certain colors. Colors when placed upon a *surface* actually seem to have a *spatial* dimension. For example, a spot of red on a flat surface seems to take a position *in front* of that surface; a spot of blue color, similarly placed, seems to *sink back* into the surface. In general, warm colors seem to advance, and cool colors seem to recede. The character of such effects, however, may be altered by differences in the value and/or intensity of the color. These spatial characteristics of color were first noted by the French artist, Paul Cézanne, in the latter part of the nineteenth century. He admired the sparkling brilliancy of the *impressionist artists* of the period but thought that their work had lost the *solidity* of earlier painting. Consequently, he began to experiment with expressing the bulk and weight of forms by modeling with *color tones*. Previous to Cézanne's experiments, the traditional, academic artist had modeled form by a *change of values* in monotone (one color). The artist then tinted over these tones with a thin, dry *local color* characteristic of the object being painted. Cézanne discovered that a *change of color* on a form could serve the purpose of a *change of value* and not lose the intensity of expression. He felt that the juicy richness of positive colors served to express the "actual" structure of a solid object. Later contemporary artists realized that Cézanne's advancing and receding colors could also create those backward and forward movements in space which give liveliness and interest to the picture surface. Many abstract artists have used the relationships of balance and movement in space to give *content* (meaning) to a painting

Colorplate 32. A three-dimensional model illustrating the three main characteristics of color. (See Figure 102)

Colorplate 33. STILL LIFE by Henri Fantin-Latour. This Still Life is painted in local color, or color which tends to describe the natural hues of the objects in nature.

Courtesy The National Gallery of Art, Washington, D.C. Chester Dale Collection.

Colorplate 34. MOTHER AND CHILD by Marie Laurencin. This French artist used color to construct a personal (or subjective) interpretation which sets the charming mood of the painting.

Courtesy The Detroit Institute of Arts, Detroit, Michigan.

Colorplate 35. STILL LIFE WITH APPLES AND PEACHES by Paul Cézanne. Cézanne uses changes of color as a means of modelling form. Cool colors are used as a means of indicating recession rather than a mere darkening of the characteristic tones.

Courtesy The National Gallery of Art, Washington, D.C. Gift of Eugene and Agnes Meyer.

Colorplate 39. FRUITS AND GUITAR by Georges Braque. The Cubist painter, Braque, commonly achieves aesthetically pleasing arrangements of color and value areas. His inventive hues are probably the choicest of early 20th-century painting and his selectivity of placement is equally significant.

Courtesy The Art Institute of Chicago.

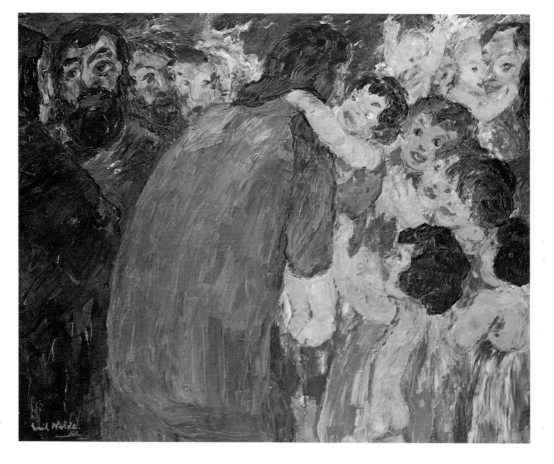

Colorplate 40. CHRIST AMONG THE CHILDREN by Emil Nolde. The Expressionists usually employed bold, clashing hues in order to emphasize their emotional identification with a subject. Intensity of feeling is created by the use of complementary and near-complementary hues.

Courtesy The Museum of Modern Art, New York. Gift of W. R. Valentiner.

Colorplate 41. PROPELLERS by Fernand Léger. Although a variety of strong colors appear in this painting, the careful repetition of a key hue (yellow) creates harmony and color balance.

Collection The Museum of Modern Art, New York. Katherine S. Dreier Bequest.

Colorplate 42. RUE A SANNOIS by Maurice Utrillo. Blue is used as a dominant hue in the painting by Utrillo. He achieves a dynamic balance by his use of smaller areas of complements and neutral white.

Courtesy Collection, Mr. and Mrs. Paul Mellon. Washington, D.C.

Colorplate 43. THE OLD PORT OF MARSEILLE by Maurice de Vlaminck. Vlaminck, another expressionist, uses the preferred contrasting hues of these emotionally inclined painters. The hues are neutralized, so that unity is achieved without loss of liveliness.

Courtesy The National Gallery of Art, Washington, D.C. Chester Dale Collection.

Colorplate 44. TWO LITTLE CIRCUS GIRLS by Auguste Renoir. Here, unity is achieved by the French artist, Renoir, through a dominantly warm color scheme in order to invoke a sense of childhood grace and charm. Although very slight traces of cool color are found in the painting, variety is basically achieved through modulations of value.

Courtesy The Art Institute of Chicago.

Colorplate 45. STILL LIFE by Paul Cézanne. Cézanne has arrived at a dominantly cool tonality in this painting, using contrasts of red and yellow in small amounts so the pattern is not disturbed.

Courtesy The National Gallery of Art, Washington, D.C. Chester Dale Collection.

Colorplate 46. CHRIST MOCKED BY SOLDIERS by Georges Rouault. Again we have an expressionist contrast of clashing complements. The pattern and harmony of the painting in this case are stabilized without loss of expression through the heavy neutralizing lines of black suggested to Rouault by medieval stained glass.

Colorplate 47. WILD FLOWERS by Odilon Redon. The use of many contrasting colors is found in this painting by Odilon Redon. The artist has brought about a pleasant relationship of these colors by employing a large area of neutral color in the background.

Courtesy The National Gallery of Art, Washington, D.C. Gift of Loula D. Lasker.

although no actual objects are represented. Color has been used as just another means along with line, value, and texture to accomplish this purpose.

Color and Emotion

A second use of color is found in its ability to create mood, to symbolize ideas, and to express personal emotions. Color itself, as found upon the canvas, may express a mood or feeling desired although it is not *descriptive* of the objects represented. Light, bright colors make us feel happy and gay while cool, dark, or sombre colors are generally depressing in character. The different hues of the spectrum may have different emotional impacts. Psychologists have found that red is happy and exciting, whereas blue may be dignified, sad, or serene. Also, different *values* and *intensities* of the hues in a color tonality may have· an effect on its *feeling tone*. A decided value range (strongly contrasting light or dark hues) gives a color scheme vitality and directness; closely related values and low intensities suggest subtlety, calmness, and repose. We cannot escape this emotional effect of color because its appeal is directly to our senses.

The artist may also take advantage of the power of color to *symbolize* ideas; thus he may make his work stronger in its content or meaning. Such ideas or abstract qualities as *virtue, loyalty, honesty, evil, cowardice* may be symbolized by the colors which have come to have a *traditional association* with them. In many cases, we do not know the origins of these associations, but are, nevertheless, affected by them. For example, blue is associated with loyalty and honesty (*true blue*), red with danger, yellow with cowardice (*yellow streak*), black with death, green with life or hope, white with purity or innocence, and purple with royalty or wealth. Some colors may have many different associations; for example, red may mean fire, danger, bravery, sin, passion, or violent death. The colors in a painting may enhance the impact of the *subject matter* by suggesting or recalling the *meanings* associated with them.

In addition to expressing meanings by association, the artist may use color to express his own *personal emotions*. Most truly creative artists evolve a personal style of color tone which comes primarily not from the subject, but from their own *feelings* about it. Albert Pinkham Ryder expressed what he felt about the sea in a very original style of color. John Marin's color is essentially *suggestive in character* with little expression of form or solidity. It is frequently delicate and light in tone in keeping with the medium (water color) with which he works. The color seen in the paintings of Vincent van Gogh is usually vivid and hot, intense in character, and applied in snaky-like ribbons of pigment. It is his use of texture and color which accounts for the intensely personal style of his work. The French artist, Renoir, used a luminous shimmering color in his painting of human flesh, so that his nudes have a glow which is not actually present in the human figure. The emotional approach to color appealed particularly to the expressionistic painter who used it to create an entirely *subjective treatment* having nothing to do with *objective reality*.

Colorplates 35, 36, 37, 38

Aesthetic Appeal of Color Tonality

The final use of color comes in its ability to invoke in the observer sensations of pleasure because of its well-ordered systems of color tonality. This appeal refers to the sense of satisfaction we get from seeing a well-designed rug or drapery materials whose color combinations are harmonious in character. The same appeal may be found in a purely nonobjective painting. There are no *exact rules* for arriving at pleasing effects in color relationship, but there are some *guiding principles* which may help us develop a feeling for them. We may develop an ability to create pleasing color by studying and analyzing color schemes which appeal to us; this study should be followed with experiment and practice in *color organization*. The problem will be, *first*, the *selection* of hues which are to be used together in a composition, and *second*, the *arrangement* of them in the pictorial field in the proper amounts for color balance. No color is important in *itself* but is always seen on the picture surface in a *dynamic interaction* with the other colors present. It must be remembered that combinations and arrangements of color are for the purpose of expressing content or meaning; consequently, any arrangement ought to have a definite *feeling tone*. In talking about pleasing color, we must realize that there can be brutal color combinations as well as refined ones; these are satisfying in the sense that they accomplish the artist's purpose of exciting us rather than having a quieting effect. Some of the German expressionist painters have proved that these brutal, clashing color schemes can have a definite aesthetic value when they are done in a purposeful manner.

color balance

Colorplate
39
In all good color combinations, there are some relationships and some contrasts. Where colors are related in *hue*, they may exhibit some contrast in *value* and/or *intensity*. The basic problem is the same one present in all aspects of form organization, *variety in unity*; there must be relationships between the color tones, but these *relationships* must be made alive and interesting through *variety*. A simple device for creating unity and balance is the *repetition* of similar color tones in different parts of the composition. An important aspect of color balance is based upon our psychological perception of complementary hues. If we look fixedly at a spot of intense red for a few moments and then shift our eyes to a white area, we will see an afterimage of the same spot in green-blue, the psychological complement. The phenomenon may be noted when *any pair* of complementary colors is used. This psychological fact is the basis for our use, in many color schemes, of a note of *complementary color* to balance the *dominating hue* used.

Colorplates
40, 41, 42
The pleasing quality of a color pattern depends frequently on the amounts or proportions of color used. In general, it may be said that *equal amounts* of different colors are not as interesting as a color arrangement where *one*

color or one kind of color *predominates*. We are often confused by color schemes where all of the tones demand equal importance because we cannot find a *dominant area* on which to fix our attention. The dominance of any one color in a pattern may be due to its hue, its value, or its intensity; it may also be affected by the character of the surrounding hues. A small, dark spot of color, through its *lower value*, may dominate over a large, light area. A spot of *intense color*, though small, may balance a larger amount of a *greyer*, more *neutralized* color. Also a small amount of warm color will usually dominate over a larger amount of cool color although both may be of the same intensity. Complementary colors, which of course vie for our attention through simultaneous contrast, may be made more attractive if one of them is softened or neutralized.

color combinations

Any attempt to base the aesthetic appeal of color pattern on certain fixed, theoretical color harmonies is not satisfactory. For one thing, the effect will depend as much on how we *distribute* our tones as it will on the *relationships* of the tones themselves. Most combinations, however, may be reduced to *two basic types* of color organization. In the first one, we depend upon the *unity of the hues* being dominant; in the second, we use hue combinations which depend for their interest on *strong contrast* and *variety* of color. Here, of course, the basic problem is to unify these contrasts without destroying the general strength and intensity of expression. In the *unified color scheme*, the opposite is true; we must introduce enough *variety of color* to keep the effect from becoming *too monotonous*. In the first type of color pattern (unity), the hue intervals are closely related as in analogous colors; in the second type (contrast), the hue intervals are further apart, the greatest possible interval being that between two complementary colors.

Unified Color Patterns. Unity is often made dominant in a color scheme by the use of *one hue only*. Naturally, variety can only be achieved in a combination of this kind by using contrasting values or intensities. This scheme may be varied by the introduction of a *small amount* of a subordinate contrasting *hue* or even a contrasting *neutral* such as white or black. Another way of relating colors where unity is desired is to *key* a number of colors toward *one hue*. This one hue will serve as a harmonizing factor if a little of it is mixed with *every color* used in the combination. The same effect may be created by glazing over a vari-colored pattern with a single tone of color, which becomes the *key color*. A third type of unified pattern is found when we use all warm or all cool colors in combination. Again, however, a small amount of a complementary or a contrasting neutral may be used for variety in the color pattern. As a rule, where warm and cool colors are balanced against each other in a composition, it is better to allow one temperature to dominate.

Contrasting Color Patterns. Color schemes based upon a strong *contrast of hue* or intensity have great possibilities for expressive effect. These contrasts may sometimes be controlled by the *amounts of contrasting color used*. Where the *basic unity* of a color pattern has been es-tablished, we may use strong contrasts of color in *small accents*; their size, then, prevents them from distributing the basic unity of the color theme. Another commonly used method of con-trolling *contrasts* is to separate all or a part of the tones by a *neutral* line or area. Absolute black or white lines are the most effective neu-trals for this purpose because they are so posi-tive in character themselves. They not only tie together the contrasting hues but serve to *en-hance their color character* because of value contrast. The use of the neutral black-leading between the brilliant colors of stained glass windows is an example of this unifying char-acter. Such modern painters as George Roualt and Max Beckman found a *black line* effective in separating their *highly contrasting* colors. A similar unifying effect can be brought about by using a large area of neutral *grey* or a *neutral-ized color* as a *background* for clashing con-trasts of color.

Finally, we should remember that combina-tions of color frequently defy the exactness of any rules and are still satisfying to the eye. The artist uses color, as he does the other elements of art structure, to give a highly personalized meaning to the *subject matter* of his work.

Colorplates 43, 44, 45, 46, 47

COLOR PROBLEMS

Problem 1

Mix with tempera paint the twelve colors, and mount in spaces as indicated on the chart.

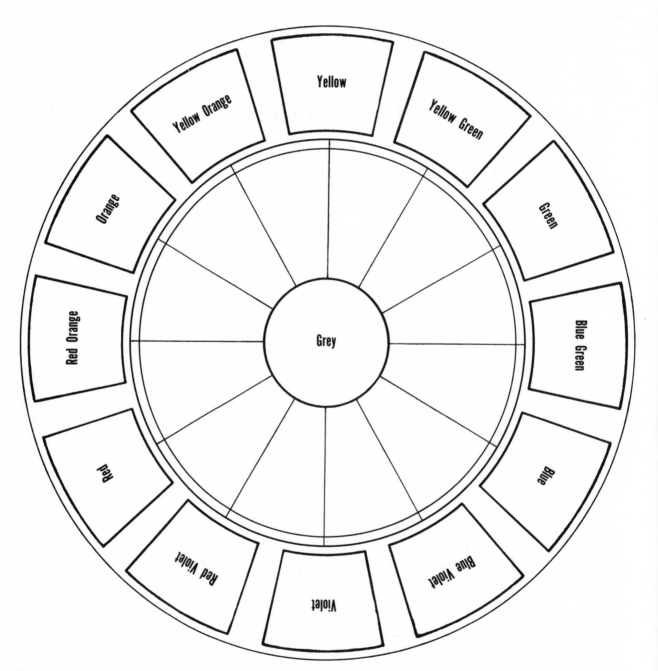

Figure 103.

PROBLEM 2

Intensity Change

Use any pair of complementary colors to create the horizontal intensity scale. At either end, the colors should be at spectrum intensity. Gradually mix a little of the complement with each color until you arrive at a neutral grey which is placed in the middle rectangle.

Value Change

In the left hand vertical column create a value scale from white to black by mixing tempera paint.

In the right hand column use any one color of the wheel at its spectrum intensity and place it next to its normal value in the neutral scale. (See chart at top of p. 90.) Mix white with this spectrum color to get the equivalent light values and match with the neutral ones of the value scale. Do the same by mixing with black to match the dark tones of the value scale.

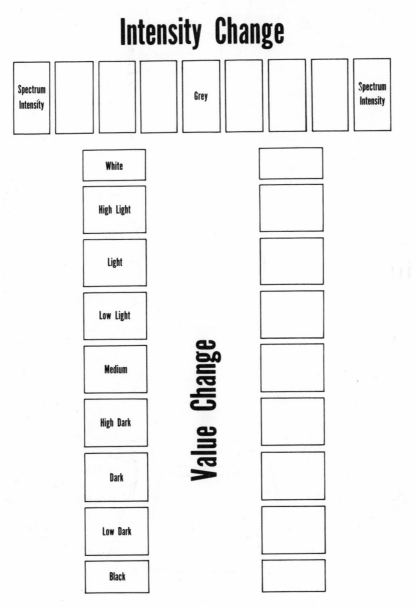

Figure 104.

PROBLEM 3

Any color may vary in appearance depending upon the color which is placed next to it. An application of the "rule of simultaneous contrast" will indicate the apparent changes in a color as it is placed against different colored backgrounds.

Make experiments in simultaneous contrast by using areas of background in the form of rectangles about 2½ by 3½ inches in size. Paste squares or circles of color about ¾ of an inch on these backgrounds.

a. Using a spot of primary or secondary color of high intensity, mount it first on a background of its complement and then on a background of any related color.
b. Use the same color in a lower intensity and mount it on the same backgrounds.
c. Use a low intensity of any primary color and mount it first on a background of plain grey or black. Then put it on a background of its own hue at a high intensity.
d. Using a neutral grey, mount it first on a background of any pure primary or secondary. Next place the same grey against a background which is the complement of the first color used.

Mount all these experiments in pairs on a large chart. Check with the text to see if the effects are the same as indicated in the section on "Rule of Simultaneous Contrast."

PROBLEM 4

The use of certain "standard" color combinations should be explored by the student. It should be noticed, however, that the use of such schemes without sensitivity to the quality and relative amounts of color used will not accomplish a satisfying result.

Lay out a page of drawing paper with five 4 by 5 inch rectangles. Within these rectangles repeat a simplified geometric design and paint each one with a different type of color combination. Use some neutrals (black, white, or grey) in each one of them. Use the following standard color schemes for this problem:

a. Monochromatic
b. Analogous
c. Complementary
d. Split-complementary (the use of one color next to the direct complement)
e. Triad (secondary or intermediate)

PROBLEM 5

Plastic use of color implies spatial relationships created by certain types of color organization. Colors which are warm in hue character and have high intensity seem to advance, whereas those which are cool and have low intensity seem to recede. Also colors which are complementary to their background seem to occupy a space in front of it.

Plan a pattern of simple planes overlapping in space. Vary the size and position of the planes in order to create interest. Cut these shapes from a variety of colored papers and paste on a background of neutral or neutralized color. Choose the colors so that they will help to establish the spatial recession of forms.

PROBLEM 6

Every color of the spectrum exists in many forms or modifications although these forms continue to bear the simple spectrum name. Modification of a color by mixing it with neutrals or even a little of its complement does not change its basic hue.

The intention of this problem is to demonstrate the many modifications which may be created from a basic color scheme. Use a simple abstract pattern created by placing a small shape and a medium size shape on a larger background area (about 2½ by 3½ inches). Choose any three contrasting colors widely separated on the color wheel and paint the design with these colors in their spectrum intensity. This represents the basic color scheme.

Using each one of these colors, see how many modifications you can make by adding varying amounts of black, white, or grey or a little of the complementary color. Paint swatches of each color modification a little larger than the original pattern. Choose a modification of each of the three original colors and combine to make a color variation of the original pattern. Make another selection to create a second variation of the pattern. Continue combining forms of the original colors until you have ten or twelve variations. (The original pattern can be created by cutting the shapes used from the color swatches and pasting them on background shapes also cut from these swatches.) Mount the original color scheme and variations in a pleasing arrangement on a large piece of illustration board. Label the original basic color pattern.

PROBLEM 7

Colors make a direct appeal to the emotions. Generally speaking such emotional states as anger, melancholy, jealousy, etc. have come to be associated with specific colors. Sensitive color employment in combination with appropriate use of the other elements of form may express greatly varied emotional feelings.

Select a black and white reproduction of a painting (or even a photograph) which seems to contain a specific mood. Reproduce this work in any medium using a color scheme expressive of that mood. Pay no attention to the naturalistic qualities of color but make sure that all other factors (particularly the light and dark pattern) are true to the work being reproduced.

PROBLEM 8

The Impressionistic painters of the 19th century developed a technical painting method to simulate the illusion of light, color, and atmosphere. Because they knew that light was composed of varying wavelengths of color, they painted surfaces with dabs of different colors placed side by side in an attempt to catch the vibrating quality of light rays. They realized that the eye would mix or fuse these colors into the variations or color mixtures which they desired.

Set up a group of simple still-life objects and draw it in simple outline form. Using tempera paint, express the quality of color in the objects by painting dots or short dabs of color on the picture surface. Instead of mixing colors on a palette, merely place them on the paper so that they will mix when the eye perceives them from a distance. For example, dots of pure green could be used with dots of blue or yellow to create modifications of hue and value. In some areas, dabs of complementary color might be used to modify the local colors seen. Dabs of cool color could be used in shadow areas to create spatial recession. It will probably be necessary to create definite value differences between forms in order that they may stand out, one from the other. Do not feel bound by rules in this problem but feel free to experiment with different tonal effects. Also, the dots of color do not have to be completely separate but may mix or overlap with each other.

PROBLEM 9

A natural subject may be interpreted by the artist in many different styles of color tonality, either unified or contrasting in hue character. As the local color character of the objects is ignored, the artist is enabled to express a personal feeling or emotional quality.

Again set up an arrangement of three or four simple still-life objects. Using any medium or combination of mediums, interpret the subject matter in several different color organizations selected from the following:

a. Strongly contrasting hues and values
b. Closely related hues and values
c. Dominant cool colors with warm accents
d. Dominant warm colors with black or white accents
e. A dark toned color scheme but with contrasting hues
f. A light toned color scheme with contrasting hues
g. Contrasting colors used with black or white lines.

Lines and textures in neutral tones may be used as decorating embellishments on, in, or around the color shapes. Areas of shadow may be ignored or considered as color shapes. Remember that the expressive quality of the color pattern is more important than the naturalistic appearance of the subject matter.

CHAPTER 9: SPACE

Definitions:

Space: The interval or measurable distance between preestablished points.

Two-dimensional Space: Measurable distances on a surface which show length and breadth but lack any illusion of thickness or depth.

Three-dimensional Space: A sensation of space which seems to have thickness and depth as well as length and breadth.

Decorative Space: A concept in which the visual elements have interval relationships in terms of a two-dimensional plane.

Plastic Space: A concept in which the visual elements on the surface of the picture plane are made to give the illusion of having relationships in depth as well as in length and breadth.

Infinite Space: A pictorial concept in which the illusion of space has the quality of endlessness found in the natural environment. The picture frame has the quality of a window through which one can see the endless recession of forms into space.

Shallow Space: This is sometimes called "limited depth" because the artist controls his use of the visual elements so that no point or form is so remote that it does not take its place in the pattern of the picture surface.

Intuitive Space: Relationships of the visual elements on the surface of the picture plane so as to give a "feeling" of the third dimension without actually giving a true illusion of solidity and depth.

Four-dimensional Space: A highly imaginative treatment of forms which gives a sense of intervals of time or motion on the picture surface.

Although *space* is not considered an element of art structure in this book, its presence is, nevertheless, felt in every work of art, presenting fundamental problems which must be faced by the artist. Space is here conceived as a *product* rather than a *tool*; it is created by the "tools" or art elements which have been discussed in the preceding chapters. The importance of space lies in its function, and a basic knowledge of its implications and use is essential to every artist. Space, as defined in this book, is limited to the graphic fields; that is, two-dimensional surface arts such as drawing, painting, printmaking, etc. The space which exists as an illusion in the *graphic* fields is actually present in the *plastic* areas of sculpture, ceramics, jewelry, and architecture.

SPATIAL PERCEPTION

All spatial implications are mentally conditioned by the environmental and experience of the viewer. Vision is experienced *through* the eyes, but *interpreted* with the mind. "Perception involves the whole pattern of nerve and brain response as well as the visual stimulus."[1] Man uses two eyes for the perception of objects in nature and continually shifts his focus of attention. In so doing, two different types of vision are used, *stereoscopic* and *kinesthetic*.

[1] Scott, Robert G., *Design Fundamentals*, McGraw-Hill Book Co., New York, Toronto, London, 1951, p. 110.

Having two eyes set slightly apart from each other, man sees two different views of the object world at the same time. The term *stereoscopic* is applied to his ability to overlap these views, which are slightly different, into one image. This visual process creates an illusion of three-dimensional depth, making it possible to judge distances.

In kinesthetic vision, man experiences space in the movements of the eye from one part of a work of art to another. Space is experienced while viewing a two-dimensional surface because we unconsciously attempt to organize its separate parts so that they can be seen as a whole. In addition, man explores object surfaces with *eye* movements in order to make *mental* recognition of them. Objects close to the eye require more ocular movement than those more distant, and this factor adds spatial illusion to man's kinesthetic vision.

TYPES OF SPACE

There are two basic types of space available to the artist; both are fundamental to spatial conception:

Decorative Spatial Concept

The graphic artist should realize that the actual surface to which he is physically limited in his art is two-dimensional and that suggestions of space, as they occur on this surface, are almost entirely a matter of premeditated illusion. The usual *picture plane* (paper, canvas, board, etc.) has height and width (see form) but no depth which could be of any significance to the artist. This depthless surface could be called *decorative space* or a space which exists *across* the plane rather than *in* it. When he adds any element of art to this blank surface plane, the artist begins to cut, divide, and rearrange the decorative space into smaller units. When this happens, the illusion of depth may appear either *accidentally* or as a result of the *intention* of the artist. The depth (or three-dimensional space) and the divisions across the surface (or two-dimensional space) are of vital concern to the artist, for they must both be organized into a coherent whole. Decorative space invariably

Figure 105. LUCKY STRIKE by Stuart Davis. Davis works with planes of intense colors generally parallel to the picture surface. Certain devices such as overlapping and transparency are employed but never in such a way as to seriously contradict the concept of flatness.

Courtesy The Museum of Modern Art, New York. Mrs. Simon Guggenheim Fund.

Figure 106. THE KNIFE THROWER, from Jazz by Henri Matisse. No depth is intended in this decorative and ornamental abstraction. The flatness of the shapes is exaggerated by avoiding modeling, but vitality is maintained by variations of contour, value, and color. A silhouetted effect is the dominant feature.

Courtesy Philadelphia Museum of Art, McIlhenny Fund.

exists in the sense that distances between images or elements can be measured *across the picture plane*; it exists only in theory in the sense that the image is completely confined to the picture plane. Thus, in terms of depth, decorative space becomes a matter of degree. Decorative space ceases when it is obvious that the artist intends to divorce the *image* from the *plane* on which it physically rests. It is doubtful that the human mind will accept the idea of a perfectly flat surface in an art work. Because of memory overlays of objective experiences, the slightest manipulation of line, value, or color will generate *an illusion of depth-space*.

Colorplate
48

Plastic Spatial Concept

The term *plastic* is applied to all images which assume the qualities of the third dimen-

sion. Man bases much of his art on his experiences in the objective world, and it is a natural conclusion that he should explore the resources of pictorial space.

deep and/or infinite space

An art work which emphasizes *deep space* denies the *picture plane* except as a starting point from which the space begins. The observer of such a work seems to be moving continuously in the far distances of the picture field. This spatial feeling will be recognized by those who have looked through an open window over a landscape which seems to roll on and on into infinity. The infinite quality of *illusionistic space* is created by the recognition of spatial indications which are produced by certain relationships of art form. Size, position,

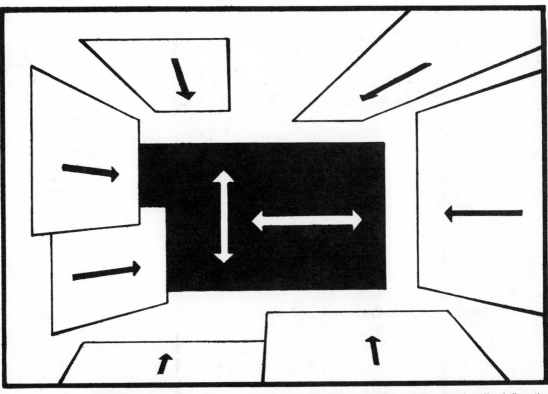

Figure 107. As a variation on the concept of shallow space, artists occasionally define the planes which make up the outer limits of a hollow box-like space behind the picture plane. The diagram shows this concept, although in actual pictorial practice a return to the picture plane would be made through objects occupying the space defined. The back plane acts significantly as a curtain which prevents penetration into deep space.

overlapping images, sharp and diminishing details, converging parallels, and perspective are the traditional methods of indicating deep spatial penetration.

Infinite spatial concepts dominated Western art from the beginning of the Renaissance (about 1350) to the middle of the nineteenth century. During this period, generations of artists such as Uccello, Botticelli, Ruisdael, Breughel, Rembrandt, Poussin, and Corot, to name only a few, developed and perfected the *deep space illusion* because of its obvious accord with *visual reality*. Present-day art is largely dominated by the *shallow space concept*, but many contemporary artists work with strongly recessed fields. Any space concept is valid if it demonstrates a consistent control of the elements in relation to the spatial field chosen.

shallow space

Artists often take an intermediate spatial position, keeping some of the qualities of deep space, but relating them to the picture plane. Awareness of the presence of the picture surface usually limits the space of a composition. Varying degrees of *limited space* are possible, ranging from the near-decorative to the near-infinite. Limited or *shallow space* could be compared to the restricted spatial feeling of a box or stage. Egyptian, Oriental, Byzantine, and medieval artists used comparatively shallow space in their works. The works of the early Renaissance were often based on shallow sculpture reliefs. In the Neoclassic paintings of Jacques Louis David, a nineteenth-century artist, most of the figure action was limited to a single plane in the foreground. David interwove his figures

Colorplate
49

decoratively on a stage-like plane which was limited by a backdrop of flat architecture.

Many modern artists have elected the use of shallow space on the theory that it admits of more positive control, and is more in keeping with the flatness of the working surface. Gauguin, Matisse, Modigliani, and Beckman, are typical advocates of the limited spatial concepts.

TRADITIONAL METHODS OF SPATIAL INDICATION

Artistic methods of spatial representation are so interwoven and interdependent that an attempt to isolate and examine all of them would be impractical and inconclusive. The illustration of all spatial means would be an interminable task and leave the reader with the feeling that art is entirely "formula-istic."

Our comprehension of space which comes to us through objective experiences is enlarged, interpreted, and given meaning by the use of our *intuitive faculties*. Spatial order develops when the artist *senses* the right balance and the best placement, and then selects vital forces to create completeness and unity. Obviously then, this process is not a purely intellectual one but a matter of instinct or subconscious response.

Since the *subjective* element plays a part in the control of space, one can readily see that emphasis on formula here, as elsewhere, can quench the creative spirit. Art is a product of man's creativity and is always dependent on individual interpretations and responses. Space,

Figure 108. BRIDE AND GROOM by Amedeo Modigliani. Modigliani dealt with simplified monumental forms given plasticity by subtle linear and value treatment and enriched by sensitive paint application. The space behind the figures is usually limited to broad severe shapes which restrict the vision of the viewer to a narrow corridor of space.

Courtesy The Museum of Modern Art, New York. Gift of Frederic Clay Bartlett.

Figure 109. ROOM INTERIOR by Jack Troutner. Many indications of space appear in this composition but they are freely varied to fit the demands of artistic unity. The sense of space is "felt" by the observer although he realizes that the indications follow no particular formula of mathematical perspective.

like other qualities in art, may be both spontaneous or premeditated, but always results as the product of the artist's will. If an artist has an impassioned will to make things so, they will usually be so, *despite inconsistency and defiance of established principles.* Therefore, the methods of spatial indication which follow are those which have been used frequently and which guarantee one effect of space, though not necessarily one which is always exactly the same. These traditional methods are presented here merely as a means of giving the student a basic conception of the more significant spatial forces.

Size

Man generally interprets largeness of scale as meaning nearness. A smaller scale conversely suggests spatial distance. If two men were to stand at distances of five and fifteen feet from us, the nearer figure would appear larger than the other. The difference of scale between the two figures would not ordinarily be understood as showing a large and small man, (although this could conceivably play a part in our perception), but as men of approximately the same size placed at varying distances from us. Therefore, if we are to use depth-scale as our guide, a figure, regardless of all other factors, must assume a scale to correspond to its distance from us. This concept of space has not always been so in art. In many broad periods and styles of art and in the works of children large scale is assigned according to importance, power, and strength, regardless of spatial location.

Colorplates
50, 51

Figure 110. THE ADORATION OF THE MAGI by Master of the Blessed Clare. The importance of the Madonna accounts for the unexpectedly large scale of her figure. This disproportionate size produces a strange conflict with the semi-realistic space with which the sizes of the angels are more in harmony. The adjustment of size to equal importance is known as "hieratic" scaling.

Courtesy Samuel H. Kress Collection, University of Miami, Joe and Emily Lowe Art Gallery, Coral Gables, Florida.

Position

For many artists and observers, there is an automatic inference that the *horizon line,* providing a point of reference, is always at the *eye level.* The position of objects is judged in relation to the horizon line; the bottom of the picture plane is seen as the closest visual point; and the degree of rise of the visual units, up to the horizon line, indicates subsequently receding spatial positions. There is evidence to suggest that this manner of seeing is instinctive (having grown out of continued exposure to the objective world), for its influence persists even in viewing greatly abstracted and nonobjective work. The alternative, of course, is to see the picture plane as entirely devoid of spatial illusion, and the distances of the visual elements actually measurable across the flat surface. It is difficult to see this way even when we discipline ourselves to do so, for it calls on us to divorce ourselves entirely from ingrained environmental factors.

Overlapping

Another way of suggesting space is by overlapping planes or volumes. If one object covers part of the visible surface of another, the first object is assumed to be nearer. The device of overlapping is a powerful indication of space, for once the device is used, it takes precedence

Figure 111.

over other spatial signs. For instance, if one ball were placed in front of another of a larger size, the overlapping ball would appear closer than the overlapped ball, despite the smaller size of the interposed sphere.

Sharp and Diminishing Detail

Because of the construction of the human eye, man is not able to see *with equal clarity* near and distant planes at the same time. A glance out the window will confirm the fact that close objects appear sharp and clear in detail; whereas, those at great distances seem blurred and lacking in definition. Artists have long been cognizant of this phenomenon and have used it widely in illusionistic work. In recent times, artists found that they could use this method and other *traditional* methods of space indication in works which were otherwise quite *abstract.* Thus, in abstract and nonobjective conceptions, sharp lines, clearly defined shapes and values, complex textures, and intense colors are associated with foreground or near positions. Hazy lines, indistinct shapes, greyed values, simple textures, and neutralized colors are identified with background locations.

Converging Parallels

The general principle of the spatial indication of converging parallels can be illustrated through the use of a rectangular plane such as a sheet of paper or a table top. By actual measurement, a rectangle possesses one set of short parallel edges and one set of long parallel edges. If the plane is arranged so that one of the short edges (A) is viewed head-on, its corresponding edge (B) will appear to be much shorter. Since these edges appear to be of different lengths, it is readily apparent that the other two edges (C and D) which connect them must seem to converge as they move back into space. Either set of lines, when separated from the other set, would continue to indicate space quite forcefully. The principle of converging parallels is found in many works of art which do not abide by the *rules of perspective.* It is closely related to perspective but it is not necessarily restrictive in a creative sense.

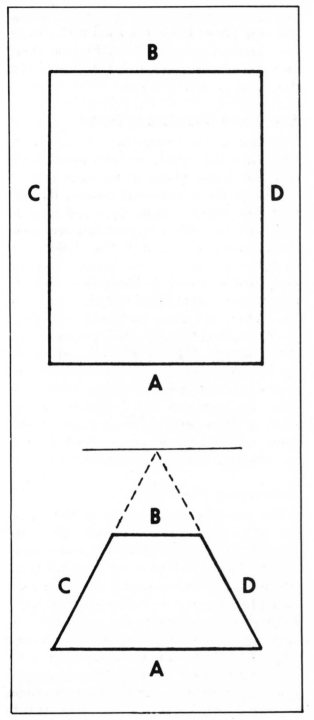

Figure 112.

Linear Perspective

Linear perspective is a geometric system used for converting sizes and distances of known objects into a unified spatial order. Its use involves the application of some of the other spatial indications such as size, position, and converging parallels. This system has been, since the Renaissance, the principal device for spatial representation in the art of the Western world.

The general understanding of perspective did not originate with the Renaissance, but the wave of scientific inquiry which swept many countries during that period brought this spatial system to a point of high refinement. The Renaissance artist focused his attention on one view, a selected portion of nature, seen from one position at a particular moment in time. The use of *vanishing points, eye-levels* and *horizon lines,* and guide lines, gave this view mathematical exactitude. To a certain extent, artists became prisoners of the system which they had helped to produce. Being a system of inflexible rules, perspective places emphasis on *accuracy of representation,* an emphasis which does not favor *creative expression.* If, however, the artist sees perspective as an aid rather than end in itself, it can be very useful to him. This attitude would conceive of perspective as something to be used, *when* and *if* the need arises, in the creation of a picture. Many fine works of art, which ignore perspective or show "faults" in the use of the system, have been and are being created. In such cases, the type of spatial order created by linear perspective simply is not compatible with the aims of the artist. Perspective then is something which should be learned by the artist simply to make it available to him.

Colorplate
52

The traditional Chinese artist could be cited as a dramatic countertype to the Renaissance artist of the West. Ancient Chinese canons prescribed convergence of parallel lines as they *approach* the spectator, creating a *reverse perspective.* This type of presentation closes the space in depth, so that the picture becomes a stage and the spectator an actor-participant in an active spatial panorama rarely losing its identification with the picture plane. Similar space concepts have been employed in the West during various historical periods. It is revealing to notice that ideas on pictorial space usually agree with the prevailing mental climate of the society which produces the art. In this sense space is a form of human expression.

SPATIAL PROPERTIES OF THE ELEMENTS OF ART STRUCTURE

As work with the elements of art structure proceeds, it becomes necessary that we recog-

nize and control the spatial effects which arise from their use. Each of the elements possesses some inherent spatial qualities, but it is the interrelationship between elements that yields the greatest spatial feeling. Many types of spatial experiences can be achieved by manipulating the elements, that is, by varying them in position, number, direction, value, texture, and color. The resultant spatial variations are endless.

Figure 113. A COURTESAN DREAMING by Kubo Shunman. The reversal of normal perspective in the table is a deliberate device used by this Japanese artist to limit the depth of space in the painting.

Courtesy The Metropolitan Museum of Art, New York. The H. O. Havemeyer Collection.

Colorplate 48. WHEATFIELDS by Jacob van Ruisdael. Early Dutch landscape painting, which aimed at the maximum illusion of visual reality, emphasized the infinite space concept. Diminishing sizes of objects and hazy effects of atmospheric perspective give the viewer a sense of seeing into far distances.

Courtesy The Metropolitan Museum of Art, New York. Bequest of Benjamin Altman.

Colorplate 49. ST. ANTHONY DISTRIBUTING HIS WEALTH TO THE POOR by Sassetta and Assistants. A shallow stage-like space is achieved in this early Renaissance painting. The work is composed in terms of two flat planes represented by the figures in front and the architectural structure in back.

Colorplate 50. SUNDAY AFTERNOON ON THE ISLAND OF LA GRANDE JATTE by Georges Seurat. The obvious progression of sizes in the figures of Seurat's painting are a strong indication of spatial recession. At the same time, these figures are carefully placed to give balance to the pattern of space and shape relationships.

Courtesy The Art Institute of Chicago.

Colorplate 51. BREEZING UP by Winslow Homer. The horizon line in this painting describes a separation of space into a ground plane below and a sky plane above. The smaller size and higher position of the distant boat helps to achieve the spatial effect.

Courtesy The National Gallery of Art, Washington, D.C. Gift of W. L. and May T. Mellon Foundation.

Colorplate 52. A DUTCH COURTYARD by Pieter de Hooch. This Dutch painting of the 17th century is an indication of the impact which the fixed perspective system of the Renaissance, 200 years previously, had upon the way artists "saw" space.

Courtesy The National Gallery of Art, Washington, D.C. Andrew Mellon Collection.

Colorplate 53. THE WATERMILL WITH THE GREAT RED ROOF by Meindert Hobbema. Concerned with the lyric qualities of landscape painting, Hobbema commonly used backlighting. This created a unified gradation of dark moving towards a light though consistently atmospheric background.

Courtesy The Art Institute of Chicago.

Colorplate 54. DYNAMIC HIEROGLYPHIC OF THE BAL TABARIN by Gino Severini. The works of the Futurists were devoted to motion for its own sake. They included not only the shapes of figures and objects, and their pathways of movement, but also their backgrounds. These features were combined in a pattern of kinetic energy.

Collection The Museum of Modern Art, New York. Lillie P. Bliss Bequest.

Line and Space

Line, through its physical structure, implies continued direction of movement, an agent for indicating spatial presence. Since, by definition, a line must be greater in length than in breadth (or else there would be difficulty in distinguishing a line from a dot or shape), it tends to emphasize one direction. The extension of this dominant direction in a single line creates continuity, moving the eye of the observer from one unit or general area to another, thus creating transition which unifies the front, middle, and background areas.

The physical properties of line contain other spatial ingredients. Long and short, thick and thin, and straight, angular, and curved lines take on different spatial positions and movements in contrast with each other. The indica-tions of three-dimensional space mentioned earlier in this chapter are actively combined with the physical properties of line. A long and thick line, for instance, will appear larger in size (a spatial indication) and hence closer to the viewer than a short and thin line. Overlapping lines establish differing spatial positions, especially when they are set in opposite directions (i.e., vertical against horizontal). In addition, the plastic qualities of such overlapping lines can be increased by modulating their values. The plastic illusion invariably suggests changes of positions in space. A single line may similarly be modulated in value and dimension to add to its plastic qualities. A diagonal line seems to move from the picture plane into deep space, whereas a vertical or horizontal line generally seems to remain comparatively static.

Figure 114. Variations of the physical properties of abstract lines can create effects of spatial recession. The thickness or darkness of value in a line may emphasize its forward position in space. Although most of the lines in this student design move across the picture plane, they occupy different positions in an imaginary space by means of differences in their sizes, values, and positions.

The spatial indication of line convergence (which occurs, subject to rule, in mechanical perspective) is always in evidence wherever a complex of lines occurs. The types of spatial suggestions arising out of this general principle are of such infinite variety that particular effects are usually the product of the artist's *intuitive* explorations. Wavy, spiral, serpentine, and zigzag line types adapt themselves to all kinds of space through their unexpected deviations of direction and accent. They seem to move back and forth from one spatial plane to another. Unattached single lines seem to define their own space and may have plastic qualities within themselves. Lines also serve to clarify the spatial dimensions of solid shapes.

Figure 115. LEUCORYX by Robert Shuler. Variation of line width suggests movement in space. When the line serves as contour for a mass, the spatial movement modifies its plastic qualities causing it to take on new dimensions.

Courtesy of the artist.

Shape and Space

In terms of space, *shape* may refer to planes, solids, or volumes, all of which occupy space and are, therefore, entitled to consideration in this chapter. A plane, which to the artist is physically two-dimensional, may create the illusion of three-dimensional space. The space appears two-dimension when the plane seems to lie on the picture surface. The space appears three-dimensional when its edges seem to converge at a point toward either the front or back of the picture plane.

Solids, volumes, or masses automatically suggest three dimensions. Such shapes express the space in which they must exist and actually become a part of it. Planes, solids, and volumes can be made to take distant positions by diminishing their size in comparison to others in the frontal picture areas, and by neutralizing their values, color, intensities, and details. This treatment relates back to the indications of space outlined earlier in the chapter.

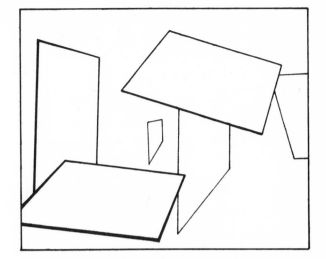

Figure 117. (2) In this example, the outlines of the two-dimensional shapes (or planes) are varied in thickness and placement, while two edges converge towards the back to give the effect of three-dimensional space. The overlapping of planes in the diagram also enhances the effect of "hollowing out" behind the picture plane.

Value and Space

The plastic effect of value can be used to control pictorial space. Light and dark spatial positions are based upon a consistent order of light source which operates reciprocally. When **Colorplate 53**

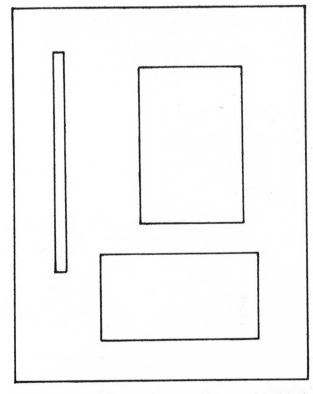

Figure 116. (1) Since the shape outlines consist of horizontals and verticals repeating the essential two-dimensional nature of the picture plane (as determined by the horizontal and verticals of the border), this diagram is an example of two-dimensional space-shape relationships.

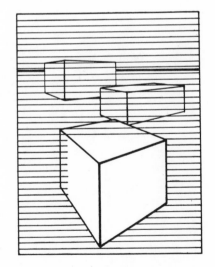

Figure 118. (3) The relationship of planes in this diagram describes an effect of solids, or volumes which in turn seem to occupy space. The size, overlapping, and placement of these volumes further increases the effect of solidity. The horizontal shaded lines are used to indicate an imaginary position for the picture plane in order to cause a projection of the near-volume into the observer's space, or in front of the picture plane.

a light source is assumed to be in *front* of a work, the objects in the foreground will appear light. The middle and background objects will become progressively darker as they move away from the picture plane. When the light source is located at the back of the work, the order of values will be reversed. The order of value change is consistent in graduation from light to dark or dark to light.

In the natural world, foreground objects are seen with clarity and great contrast while distant objects are ill-defined and grey. Therefore, neutral greys, when juxtaposed with blacks or whites, will generally take distant positions.

Cast shadows are sometimes helpful in describing plastic space, but may be spatially confusing and even injurious to the design if they are not handled judiciously.

It is very important to notice that *value-modeling can be abstract* in the sense that it need not follow the *objective natural order* of light and dark. Many artists have totally ignored this natural order, using instead the inherent spatial positions resulting from the *contrasts of dark and light.*

Figure 119. DELIGHTS OF THE POET by Giorgio de Chirico. Cast shadows in this work function psychologically and spatially. The stark shadows suggest a melancholy time between night and day and emphasize the loneliness of the scene by exaggerating the immensity of the existing space.

Courtesy The Museum of Modern Art, New York. The Lillie P. Bliss bequest.

Texture and Space

Because of the surface enrichment which texture produces, it is frequently a temptation to think of this element purely in terms of *decorative* usefulness. Actually, texture functions *plastically* by describing the depth position of surfaces. Generally speaking, sharp, clear, and bold textures seem to advance, while fuzzy, dull, and minuscule textures recede. Textures, when modified through varied use of value, color, and line, should function as a significant contribution to the total pictorial unity.

Textures are some of the visual signs used to produce the decorative surface so valued by contemporary art. The physical character of textures is related to allover patterned designs and, as such, operates effectively on decorative surfaces. When patterned surfaces are repeated and distributed over *the entire pictorial area,* the *flatness* of the picture plane becomes of vital importance. The works of Pablo Picasso frequently illustrate the contemporary use of texture surfaces to preserve the concept of *the flat picture plane.*

Figure 120. SEATED WOMAN by Pablo Picasso. Abstract textures because of their obviously decorative quality emphasize the flatness of the picture plane. Background and foreground forms become closely integrated so that little sense of spatial recession is felt by the observer.

Courtesy The Art Gallery of Ontario, Toronto, Canada.

Color and Space

One of the outstanding contributions of the modern artist has been his reevaluation of the plastic potentialities of color. Color is now integrated directly into the form of the picture by using it in a positive and direct manner to model the various spatial planes of surface areas (see Chapter VIII, The Uses of Color). Since the time of Cézanne, a new awareness of the advancing characteristics of color is evident in art. Prior to this time, deep space was considered as beginning *with* the picture plane and *receding from it*. Today many artists, chiefly through the use of color, deal with the spaces on or *in front* of the picture plane. Piet Mondrian, the Dutch geometric abstractionist, used intense colors to advance shapes *beyond the picture plane*.

Analogous colors, through their relationships, create spatial movement, and contrasting colors provide varied accents or focal points of interest. Both are used to exploit the limitless dimensions of space.

RECENT CONCEPTS OF SPACE

Every great period in the history of art has espoused a particular "type" of space conception. These spatial preferences reflected basic conditions within the civilizations which produced them. Certain fundamental space attitudes seem to recur in varied forms throughout recorded history. During the period of their influence, these attitudes become a "norm" of vision for the people, gradually conditioning them to see things in much the same way. As a new space attitude is ushered in by epic social changes, it is usually resisted until this new image, in turn, becomes the standard filter through which people see things. These changes were fairly cyclical and even predictable through the Renaissance. The acceleration of change prompted by the cataclysmic revelations of modern science has today produced new concepts which are without precedent. The artist is today groping for ways of understanding and interpreting these ever-widening horizons, and, as he does, his explorations are met by the characteristic recalcitrance of the public.

Search for a New Spatial Dimension

The artist of the Renaissance, conditioned by the outlook of the period, set as his goal the optical, scientific mastery of nature. He sought to accomplish this by reducing nature, part by part, to a *static geometric system*. By restricting his attention to one point of view, the artist was able to develop perspective and represent some of the illusionary distortions of actual shapes as seen by the human eye.

The modern artist, equipped with the finding of new scientific and industrial materials and technology, has extended the search into nature initiated by the Renaissance. He has probed into nature's inner and outer structure with the microscope, camera and telescope; with the car and the airplane, he has had an opportunity to see more of the world than any of his predecessors. The radically changed environment of the artist has brought about a new awareness of space. It has become increasingly evident that the essence of space cannot be described from the one point of view characteristic of the Renaissance, and a continuing search has been instituted for a new graphic vocabulary to describe visual discoveries. Since one outstanding feature of the modern world is motion, new artistic representations must move, at least illusionistically. Motion has become *a part of space*, and this space can be grasped only if a certain *period of time* is allotted to cover it. Hence, a new dimension is added to spatial conception; often referred to as the fourth dimension, the elements of space, time, and motion have presented an important graphic challenge. This challenge is the discovery of a practical method for the representation of things in motion from every viewpoint on a flat surface. In searching for solutions to this problem, the artist has turned to his own experiences as well as the work of others.

plastic image

Paul Cézanne, the nineteenth-century Post-Impressionist, was an early pioneer in the attempt to express this new dimension. His aim was to render objects in a manner more true to nature. This nature, it should be pointed out, was not the Renaissance world of optical appearances; instead, it was a world of forms in space, conceived in terms of a plastic image. In painting a picture of a still life, Cézanne would select *the most characteristic viewpoints* of all his objects; he would then change the eye levels, split the individual object planes, and combine all of these views in *the same painting* creating a composite view of this group. Cézanne would often shift his viewpoint of a single object from the right side to the left side, and from the top to the bottom, always creating the illusion of *looking around the object.* If one wished to see these multiple views, one would be forced to move around the object or revolve it in front of him. This act would involve *motion, space* and *time*.

The *cubists* adopted many of Cézanne's pictorial devices. They usually showed the object from as many views as suited the discrimination of the artist. Objects were rendered in a type of *orthographic drawing,* in which the basic intention was division into essential views which could be drawn in *two dimensions.* The basic view is called a *plan,* one which might be thought of as the top view. Using the plan as a basis, the *elevations* (or profiles) were taken from the front or back and the *sections* from the right and left sides. The juxtaposition of these views in a painting illustrated the *movement of the objects in space.* Such a painting was a composite which showed much more of the object than would normally be visible. The

Figure 121. ORANGES by Paul Cézanne. Cézanne was concerned with the plastic reality of forms as well as their organization into a unified design. Although the plate, jar, and pot are present in the same picture they are depicted as seen from different viewponts. For example, he felt that the plate would seem to have greater reality if drawn as seen from a higher angle; on the other hand, the jar placed behind this object seems to be observed from a lower viewpoint.

Courtesy The Museum of Modern Art, New York. Lillie P. Bliss Collection

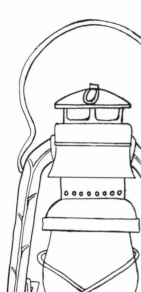

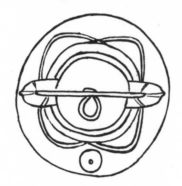

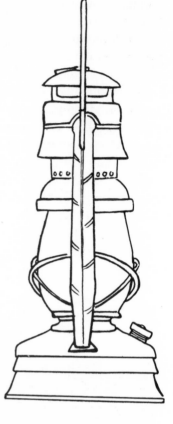

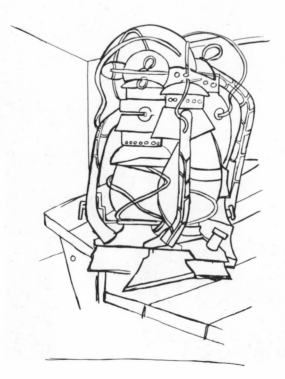

Figure 122. KEROSENE LAMP by Tom Haverfield. This student work illustrates the following excerpt from the text—"Objects were rendered in a type of orthographic drawing, in which the basic intention was division into essential views which could be drawn in two dimensions. The juxtaposition of these views in a painting illustrated the movement of the objects in space. Such a painting was a composite which showed much more of the object than would normally be visible."

technique seems a "distortion" to the lay spectator conditioned to a static view although within the limits of artistic selection, everything is present which one would ordinarily expect to see.

In the works of the cubists, we find the suggestion that a picture can have a life of its own, and that the creation of space is not essentially a matter of portrayal or rendering. Step by step the cubist works illustrate that the greater the departure from *object resemblance,* the clearer the *spatial order* may become. One of the offshoots of this discovery was the synthetically-designed picture, or one which divorces itself from the model.

Figure 123. THE CHESSBOARD by Juan Gris. Spatial movements formed in abstractly designed paintings give variety and interest to the pattern relationships. Natural spatial indications are ignored in favor of a more subjective interpretation of the objects represented.

Courtesy The Museum of Modern Art, New York.

pictorial representations of movement in time

From time immemorial, artists have grappled with the problem of the representation of movement on the stationary picture surface. In the works of prehistoric and primitive man, the efforts were not organized, but isolated attempts to show a limited phase of observed movement.

Greek sculptors organized the lines in the draperies of their figures to accent *a continuous*

direction. By means of this device, the eye of the observer is directed along a constant edge or line. This was an early attempt to add movement or otherwise static figures.

The artists of the Medieval and Renaissance periods illustrated the life and passion of Christ by repeating a series of still pictures. The representation of the different phases of Christ's life (either in sequence form or combined in a single work) created a visual synopsis of His movement, the space He covered and the time

Colorplate
54

Figure 124. LEASH IN MOTION by Giacomo Balla. In the effort to conceive a solution to the problem of suggesting motion as it is involved in time and space, Balla invented the idea of repeated contours. This soon became a device commonly imitated in newspaper "comic-strips," thus losing aesthetic uniqueness.

Courtesy George F. Goodyear and the Buffalo Fine Arts Academy.

He took to cover it. These pictures were the antecedents of the modern comic and motion picture techniques which actually fill the gaps between the still views in the final product.

Another representational device used for the suggestion of movement is the superimposition of many stationary views of the figure or its parts in a single picture. This device catalogs the sequence of positions of a moving body, indicating the visible changes of movements.

Twentieth-century artists have attempted to fuse the different positions of the figure by filling out the pathway of its movements. Figures are not seen in fixed positions but as *moving paths of action*. The subject in Marcel Duchamp's "Nude Descending a Staircase" is not the human body but the type and degree of energy it emits as it passes through space. This painting signified important progress in the pictorialization of motion because the plastic forces are *functionally integrated with the composition*.

The works of the Futurists (see Futurism, Chapter X) were devoted to motion for its own sake. They included not only the shapes of figures and objects, and their pathways of movement, but also their backgrounds. These features were combined in a pattern of kinetic energy. Although this expression was not entirely new as a form of expression, it provided a new type of artistic adventure, simultaneity of figure, object, and environment.

The exploration of space in terms of the four-dimensional space-time continuum is in its infancy. As research reveals more of the mysteries of the natural world, art will continue to absorb and apply them according to their effect on human relationships. It is not unreasonable to assume that even more revolutionary concepts will emerge in time, producing great changes in art style. The important thing to remember is that "distortions" and unfamiliar forms of art expression do not occur in a vacuum—that they usually represent earnest efforts to apprehend and interpret our world in terms of the latest frontiers of understanding.

Figure 125. NUDE DESCENDING A STAIRCASE, No. 2 by Marcel Duchamp. "The subject in Marcel Duchamp's painting is not the human body but the type and degree of energy it emits as it passes through space."

Courtesy Philadelphia Museum of Art. The Arensberg Collection.

SPACE PROBLEMS

PROBLEM 1

In conjunction with linear perspective, artists of the past frequently used diminishing contrasts of hue, value and intensity of color and texture to achieve a deep penetration of space on a two-dimensional surface. This is known as the infinite concept of space or atmospheric perspective.

Create a pictorial composition based on the theme, "objects in space." Conceive of the picture plane as the near side of a volume of deep space. Use the indications of space suggested in the opening paragraph, plus softening edges of objects as they are set back in depth. The human figure may be used to help suggest the scale of objects in space. Foreground, middle ground, and deep space may be indicated by size of similar objects.

PROBLEM 2

Certain artists of the past, particularly the Egyptians, conceived of space in art as a two-dimensional arrangement. In effect, objects to be shown were placed vertically above one another or side by side. This is essentially a decorative space concept.

Attempt to keep the sense of the picture plane by eliminating all signs of three-dimensional space, such as diminishing hue, value, and intensity of color or texture. Utilize objects such as those in Problem 1, but attempt to give the appearance that they lie upon and are a part of the surface of the picture. This is essentially a two-dimensional problem in semiabstract patterns.

Figure 126.

PROBLEM 3

Many artists today prefer some of the qualities of design provided by a decorative space concept but wish to retain some suggestion of three-dimensional depth.

a. Without radically altering the two-dimensional surface of the picture plane, create a semi-abstract form using some of the spatial tools in Problem 1. i.e. gradation in size, placement in picture plane, overlapping, transparency, open or closed composition, closely related hues, values, and brightness. The effect created should be of a measurable depth; i.e., as if the furthest penetration into the space back of the picture plane were a few inches rather than infinite depth.

b. In this problem, conceive of the space back of the picture plane as somewhat similar to the effect of Problem 3a, but with the side planes, top plane, and ground plane as well as the back plane clearly defined by color, value, texture or other means. Movements in depth should be resolved by returning them to the foreground through various devices. Use planes and solids to give form and pattern to the enclosed space. The concern is primarily with space itself in this problem, as contrasted to the relationship of objects in space found in Problem 1.

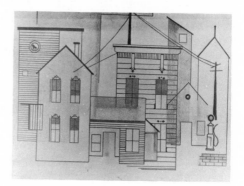

Figure 127.

PROBLEM 4

Interior space problems have frequently been solved in varied ways by artists.

In this problem, conceive of an interior of enormous proportions defined by objects lighted from a fixed position in the space, a great railway or air terminal lighted by windows in the roof. The effect should be similar to Problem 1 and Problem 3b combined.

PROBLEM 5

There are varying ways of organizing objects in space. The following problems represent two variations of space organization.

a. Utilizing either abstract solids or realistic objects, organize the resultant volumes into a diagonal series of movements penetrating into semi-deep space.

b. Create a similar space composition organizing the volumes into a circle, or a series of circles in space.

Figure 128.

PROBLEM 6

Many artists consider the unfilled portions of space as important as the solids occupying the space.

Beginning with objects such as those in a still-life set-up or a landscape, define either a fairly deep or shallow space by emphasizing the hollows (negative areas) around and between the objects through the use of devices such as value, texture, and color. The result should be an abstraction which is concerned with the importance of hollow areas in any kind of spatial organization as opposed to the attention to volumes in Problem 5a and b.

PROBLEM 7

Many contemporary artists consider transparency an important way of defining space.

Using linear perspective or parallel convergence of lines, create the effect of looking through transparent planes set at different angles to one another within a volume of space. Define several different distances in depth by making some planes opaque or semi-transparent with color, texture, value or combinations of these elements.

PROBLEM 8

Obviously decorative textures are visual signs often used by the contemporary artist to limit spatial indication. These decorative relationships permit a more free interpretation of object shapes and permit variations which can contribute to organic unity of the pictorial elements. The result is a shallow or decorative space concept.

Create a composition of forms derived from a still-life group in the studio or from a sketch of architectural forms. Omit indications of naturalistic light-and-shade substituting decorative textures of lines, spots, stripes, etc. Break up background areas into arbitrary shapes which seem related to objects and use treatments of decorative texture in some of these spaces as well. Solid tones of varying values and/or color may be used to keep the overall design from becoming too "busy" and overelaborate in character.

Figure 129.

PROBLEM 9

Cézanne and the Cubists often combined several viewpoints of a plastic image in one painting. The juxtaposition of multiple views in a single painting implies the movement of the observer around the objects.

Select a single object to be used as a model for this problem. On three pieces of tracing paper, draw the top or plan view, the elevation of profile view, and a section view of the same object to the same scale. Place these drawings one over another and combine in a single work the most characteristic parts of each view. Add value differences for contrast, variety and enhancement of spatial position.

PROBLEM 10

An early representational device for suggesting movement, as used by twentieth-century artists was the superimposition of stationary views of a figure or its parts in a single picture.

a. Select a moving figure or object as a model. Draw a series of pictures representing this figure or object as it rotates, tilts or falls in space. Each of the drawings should indicate a slight change of movement in space or position. Superimpose and place the drawings together in such a way as to suggest a continuous movement in space. This problem is not intended to create a complete pictorial organization but is an experiment in representing movement on a flat surface.

b. Select parts of the sequence of motion referred to in the above experiment. Combine these within the limits of a frame-shape so as to create an organized pattern. Add value differences for contrast, variety and enhancement of spatial position.

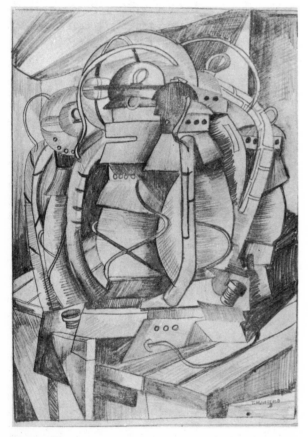

Figure 130.

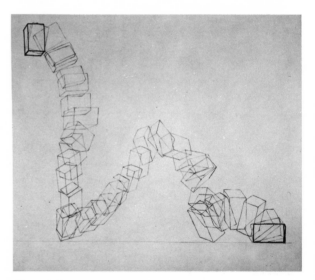

Figure 131.

PROBLEM 11

Varying sizes of forms and their positions in relationship to each other and to the planes in picture space are traditional methods of space indication.

Make a contour drawing of a human figure which is reasonably accurate as to proportion but greatly simplified in detail. Repeat this drawing about twelve times on a sheet (or sheets) of light grey construction paper varying the sizes of the figures dramatically.

Cut the figures out and place them on a 9″x12″ sheet of white paper which has had a horizontal line drawn across it at an elevation of approximately 6″.

Using this line as an indication of the horizon, place the figures in locations appropriate to their sizes in terms of distance. Some figures should be isolated and others gathered together to form groups .Make the figures overlap occasionally to accent spatial differences. Mix up the sizes in figure groups and note the variations in figures which are in proximity. Give the illusion of difference in stature as well as depth-distance (i.e. the figures would seem to indicate various age-levels).

Note—Linear Perspective is a mechanical technique of optical illusionism which produces a standardized spatial effect based on the single viewpoint of the observer-artist. Many art teachers believe, and with some justification, that the inherent dangers in perspective outweigh its value. Others feel that it is an established form of vision and, as such, deserves some consideration even though there may be violent disagreement on the desirable depth of instruction. The authors believe that there is some legitimacy to both of these views. The intricacies of perspective are too great to be covered successfully in this volume. Consequently problems are omitted, and the extent of study in this phase of art is left to the judgment of the individual instructor. If this book is not being used in connection with classroom work, the reader is advised to seek further information on perspective in works which deal specifically with the subject.

CHAPTER 10: FORMS OF EXPRESSION

DEFINITION OF EXPRESSION

The fixing of an image, whether it be in the form of oil pigment on canvas or pencil upon drawing paper, is only one aspect of the act of artistic creation. The character or personality of this formal image is determined as much by the artist's mental and emotional response to subject matter as by his choice of media and manipulation of tools. Kepes says:

"The image grows in the sense that man sees what he wants to see. As each tool has its own unique way of living on the picture surface, so each individual has his own way of binding optical signs into shapes and images that he would like to see."[1]

Expression in art is primarily concerned with the intangible quotient of creativity previously mentioned in the chapter, "The Nature of Art." It is this unique creative urge and its formal crystallization which art critics consider when making distinctions between ordinary artists and those who are truly marked with genius.

The artist may be said to express his "feelings" about life growing out of his continuing experiences with people, places, events, objects, and ideas. These experiences, interwoven with the associations and sentiments in memory, are molded or reworked in the mind through the artist's understanding of artistic values. Finally, this "feeling image" is given *form* and *meaning* through the artist's mastery of his chosen medium. Expression becomes the stylistic *form* in which the artist couches his sensuous-visual *meaning*; it is an attempt to say something about his *subject* in terms of his own time. Expression is thus directly related to the basic components of a work of art.

CLASSIFICATION OF EXPRESSION AS STYLISTIC FORM

There are two broad classifications of *expression* as stylistic form: *individual* and *group*. Group expressions are those of a society as a whole coming into being and achieving sophistication with the birth and growth of its culture. An example of group expression would be the development in ancient Greek civilization of "idealism" wherein the artist saw "humanity transfigured by its destiny."[2] Within such a group expression, social changes will affect its *style* so that quite discernible variations of attitude toward *subject, form,* and *meaning* may take place. These variations could be traced from the lively *conceptualism* of early Greece (seventh century B.C. to early fifth century) through the refined *perceptualism* of the Classic Age (late fifth century to fourth century B.C.) to the Hellenistic Age (fourth through the third century B.C.) when there is a gradual loss of

---

[1]Kepes, Gyorgy, *Language of Vision,* Paul Theobald & Co., Chicago, 1951, p. 194.
[2]Seltman, Charles, *Approach to Greek Art,* The Studio Publications, London, New York, 1948, p. 63.

Colorplate 55. THE ARAB TAX by Eugene Delacroix. A subject matter offering violent action located in exotic foreign settings was often found in paintings of the Romantic movement. Although relaxed in style, interpretation was generally bold in technique with an emphasis on the selection of bright colors.

Courtesy The National Gallery of Art, Washington, D.C. Chester Dale Fund.

Colorplate 56. KEELMEN HEAVING COALS BY MOONLIGHT by **Joseph Turner.** The historical origin of theme and semi-narrative presentation of subject represent qualities found in many works of the Romantic movement. In his manner of using color to produce atmospheric effects, Turner anticipated the techniques of the later Impressionists. Like these artists, he placed less emphasis on formal organization.

Courtesy The National Gallery of Art, Washington, D.C. Widener Collection.

Colorplate 57. MAX SCHMITT IN A SINGLE SCULL by Thomas Eakins. The Naturalist artists were Realists who became more interested in particularizing people and events by a carefully descriptive style of expression. The oarsmen are here minutely described by the artist in terms of specific people taking part in a particular activity and in a particular setting.

Courtesy The Metropolitan Museum of Art, New York. Alfred N. Punnett Fund and Gift of George D. Pratt.

Colorplate 58. BANKS OF THE SEINE, VETHEUIL by Claude Monet. The selection of subject in this painting is typical of the Impressionist movement. The bright scene and the shimmering water offered opportunity for the expression of light and atmosphere through a scientific approach to the use of colors.

Courtesy The National Gallery of Art, Washington, D.C. Chester Dale Collection.

Colorplate 59. FOUR DANCERS by Edgar Degas.
Two aspects of the Impressionist artist's recording
of natural form may be found in the painting of four
dancers. First, it demonstrates the customary interest in the effects of light (although in this case we
find an interior lighting rather than sunlight in the
out-of-doors); in addition, it shows a high angle viewpoint of composition derived from Japanese prints
or from the accidental effects characteristic of
photography.

Courtesy The National Gallery of Art, Washington, D.C.
Chester Dale Collection.

**Colorplate 60. THE MOON AND THE EARTH by Paul
Gauguin.** Color and form are here freely interpreted
to suggest the naive qualities of an uncivilized people; the relationships of these elements are expressed in terms of an over-all decorative structure
which adds to the general effect of tranquility.

Collection The Museum of Modern Art, New York. Lillie P.
Bliss Collection.

Colorplate 61. CYPRESSES by Vincent van Gogh. This highly personal style exaggerates the organic forces of nature and makes them dramatically expressive. The heavy, swirling applications of paint enhance the movements extracted from the natural form.

artistic values in favor of purely associational, imitative, and academic qualities.

The individual expressiveness in the handling of subject matter, form, and content seems more appropriate to our own time than the group expressions of the past. This is probably due to our present-day extollation of self-assertion and individualism. Although general groupings or categories of artists with similar intentions may be made in the art of the nineteenth and twentieth centuries, hosts of variations within these basic directions are discernible. The contemporary accent on individuality has resulted in a greater diversity of artistic expression since mid-nineteenth century than is found in art previous to that time.

Through a summarization of the movements in the art of today, we can be made to realize that the traditions of the past have not suffered wholesale rejection. Actually these traditions have been merely reevaluated in the light of modern tastes. The changing concepts of physical beauty down through ages illustrate the fact that each period has its own standards of taste —women in paintings by Rubens look rather "bulky" when seen in comparison with those who fit our modern concept of fashion-figure slimness. In a like manner, certain artists of the past, who were once rejected, are now preferred to many others; occasionally, even a whole artistic tradition, once considered of great significance, may be relegated to a lower level of consideration. No tradition of the past, whatever its direction, should be completely rejected, as we can find something of beauty or quality in all of them. It is essentially a matter of orienting ourselves to "see" those qualities in the same way that their creator was able to "see" them. It is this manner of "seeing" which explains why once-rejected traditions are now wholly acceptable and even preferred to those which were at one time considered to be of greater significance.

The varied forms of expression in contemporary art may be accounted for through studying the psychological and sociological changes that occurred in the late nineteenth- and early twentieth-century art. The scope of this book will not permit us to completely explore these backgrounds, so we have limited this chapter to a simplified accounting of the successive movements and attempted to explain their primary artistic aims. Many fine books and articles giving a more complete treatment are available to challenge the student who wishes to explore these backgrounds more deeply.

Nineteenth-Century Forerunners of Twentieth-Century Art

All of the forms of expression in nineteenth-century art have contributed in some degree to the character of art movements in the present century. Surprisingly, twentieth-century art, in general, may be considered a reaction to all art since the latter half of the eighteenth century. Without a background of understanding, it becomes impossible to see the art of today as a development of that produced in the past.

Until the middle of the last century, artists were still directly inspired by the visual appearance of the world around them. With the invention of the camera, however, science disposed of difficulties remaining to the imitation of natural appearance. By this time, artists as well had so completely solved the problem of representing reality that they were compelled to search for new directions of expression. Some turned toward introspection in their search for new forms; others looked toward a reevaluation of concepts of artistic form which prevailed prior to the Renaissance. These included the ideals of ancient Greek art, forms of expression used by primitive man, and styles characteristic of the medieval period. The opportunity to examine photographs of hitherto unknown art manners (Oriental art and that of the American Indian) provided a background for the evolution of new directions.

Economic influences, many of which still affect the art of today, also played a part in this search for new principles of expression. For the past two hundred and fifty years, the artist had depended for his economic welfare on the patronage of a wealthy clientele. Rather than asserting their own inventiveness and individuality, artists had gradually adopted the less

Figure 132. OATH OF THE HORATII by Jacques Louis David. A cold, formal ordering of shapes with emphasis on the sharpness of drawing characterized the neoclassic form of expression. Both style and subject matter seemed to be derived from ancient Greek and Roman sculpture.

Courtesy The Toledo Museum of Art, Gift of Edward Drummond Libbey. Toledo, Ohio.

aesthetic viewpoint of their patrons, the wealthy aristocrats and burghers. Many artists were content to supply works of art which were designed to satisfy and flatter the vanity of their patrons. A few great artists naturally evaded such bonds of artistic degradation and drew their inspiration from the society around them as well as from universal meanings.

neoclassicism

The earliest new principle—actually a rediscovery of older intentions in art—was an attempt to seek freedom from this economic bondage.

A reaction to the earlier "patronized" form of art resulted in the formation of formalized institutions such as the French Academy. The art of the Academy was characterized by rules for achieving "correct" works of art which contained "messages" of a high moral order. Artists involved in this Neoclassic movement at the beginning of the nineteenth century did not reject patronage so much as they rejected the class of people who had patronized the artist of the eighteenth century. Such prominent artists as Jacques Louis David and Jean Auguste Ingres may be seen as largely replacing the patronage of the effete French aristocracy with that of the Napoleonic state and the upper middle class.

romanticism

The first group of artists to reject any kind of servitude to a patron, or even to a class of patrons, were the Romantics. They may be considered the first revolutionaries of modern times because of their concern with the work of art itself rather than its significance to a patron or even to an observer. The true revolutionary realizes that he does not have to seek an audience; if he has something worthwhile to say, people will eventually be convinced of his viewpoint.

This has become one of the fundamental principles underlying the creative art of our time. As a result of this revolt, the artist has based his expression on his own inspiration and his study of past traditions; he is again tuned to the world of all human experience. However, in this world, the artist has found many contradictions; as a result, we find many contradictions in the art of today.

The most important artists of the Romantic group were: Eugene Delacroix in France, Francisco Goya in Spain, Joseph M. Turner in England, and Albert Pinkham Ryder in America. Illustrations of the paintings of some of these men will show the characteristics of the movement.

Colorplate 55

Figure 133. EL FAMOSO AMERICANO by Francisco Goya. The Romanticism of Goya is here displayed both in his choice of subject matter and a characteristic dramatic use of light-and-dark values.

Courtesy Philadelphia Museum of Art.

Figure 134. ADVICE TO A YOUNG ARTIST by Honoré Daumier. Influenced by a climate of scientific positivism, the artists of the Realist movement strived toward a recording of the world as it appeared to the eye but with interpretations which contained overtones of timeless quality. This painting by Daumier suggests not so much a particular appearance of costume and setting but a universal quality in the subject—the "idea" that the working people of all ages have had similar qualities.

Courtesy National Gallery of Art, Washington, D.C. Gift of Duncan Phillips.

realism and naturalism

Where the art of the Romantics had been a reaction to the pseudo-classic, academic formulas of Neoclassicism, the Realist movement was a reaction against the exotic escapism and literary tendencies of Romantic art. Wishing to avoid the pretentious attitudes of the previous group and stimulated by the prestige of science, the Realists wanted to show the world as they thought it appeared to the average layman. Although attempting to avoid mere surface appearances, they wanted to give a sense of immediacy which they found missing in the idealizing expression of Romantic and Neoclassic artists. A related group, now known as Naturalists, wanted to go beyond the results achieved by the Realists. Their attempts to make a visual copy of nature, exact in all its minute details, were probably influenced by the results obtained with the newly-invented camera.

impressionism

In the nineteenth-century movement of Impressionism, we find a strong shift toward the contemporary view in art; the *form* of the work of art (materials and methods) is emphasized rather than significant *subject matter* from nature. Where previous movements had developed the trend toward freedom of choice in subject matter, the Impressionists contributed a new technical approach to painting; this stressed the artist's interest in the appearance of his work, in terms of form, as much as it did the appearance of nature. Impressionism represents the transition between tradition and revolution. The Impressionists still wished to show nature in its most characteristic way but were mildly revolutionary in using technical aids to represent special conditions of light and atmosphere.

The Impressionist's interest in the illusion of light and atmosphere required an intensive study of the scientific light theory of color and the effect of light on the color of objects. They discovered the principle of juxtaposing complementary colors in large areas for greater brilliance; they interpreted shadows as composed of colors complementary to the hue of the object casting those shadows. To achieve the vibratory character of light, they revived the old principle of *tache* painting, a technique in which the pigment is put on the canvas in thick spots which catch actual light and reflect it from the surface. The tachist method of painting seems to have been invented by the Venetians of the sixteenth century and may be seen in the work of Titian; later applications of the style may be found in the painting of Hals, Goya, and Constable. The Impressionists employed the style in a new way by using complementary hues in the dabs of pigment; when seen at a distance, these tend to form fused tones from the separate hues.

Colorplates 56, 57, 58

Local colors became all important to the Impressionists, because their whole intent was to capture the transitory effects of sunlight and shadow, or of any kind of weather condition. Landscape became the favorite subject matter of the Impressionist painter, because of this variability of local colors under changing weather conditions.

Traditional ways of artistic interpretation underwent a second alteration when the Impressionists discovered the fascinating possibilities of unexpected angles of composition. The new photographic views of the natural scene were often different from the conventional arrangements used by artists for many years. This attitude was also partially encouraged by the character of oriental block prints which were being imported into France for the first time. These prints were often cropped down for shipment to Europe; as a result, many had curious, truncated compositions which seemed unique to western artists.

Colorplate 59

Artists representative of Impressionism in France about 1870 were Claude Monet, Camille Pissarro, Auguste Renoir, and sometimes Edgar Degas. There were deficiencies in Impressionist theory which caused some artists in the group to separate and pursue their own directions. One of the principal deficiencies was the loss of structural form resulting from the acceptance of surface illusion alone. A second was related to the effect which outdoor lighting has on the way an artist sees color; in strong sunlight, it was difficult to avoid making greens too raw, and there was a tendency to overload the canvas with yellows.

post-impressionism

Late in the nineteenth century, artists who had once been inspired by Impressionist theories began to abandon many of the principles of the movement. The most important artists in this reaction were Paul Cézanne, Paul Gauguin, and Vincent van Gogh; from these three pioneers stem the major expressions or directions of twentieth-century art.

The group has been later classified under the term, Post-Impressionism, an ambiguous title meaning "following Impressionism." This vague title does not satisfactorily indicate the far-reaching objectives of the artists in the movement. These artists sought (1) a return to the structural organization of pictorial form, (2) an emphasis on decorative organization for the sake of unity as well as the enchanting patterns which might result, and (3) a more or less conscious use of exaggerations of natural appearance for emotionally suggestive effects (commonly called *distortion*). Cézanne may be said to represent primarily the first of these aims, Gauguin, the second, and Van Gogh, the third; each, however, had some aspect of the other's objectives incorporated in his form of expression. It was these similarities which cause them to be grouped under one movement although, unlike the Impressionists, they worked independently toward their goals.

Colorplate
60

Cézanne was the dominant artist in the Post-Impressionist movement. In a manner contrary to the haphazard organization and ephemeral forms of the Impressionists, he saw a work of art in terms of an interrelationships of all of its parts. He retained the individual color spots of the former group, but in his painting these became building blocks in the total physical structure of the work. Although he may be called an *analyst* of reality rather than a *recorder* of reality (like the Impressionists and Naturalists), he goes beyond mere analysis.

Colorplate
61

Reality, for him, was not the object in nature from which he drew his inspiration, but rather represented all of the artistic conclusions arrived at in the completed work. He conceived of reality as the totality of expression derived from the appearance of nature as it became transformed under the artist's hand. Therefore, although Cézanne found his beginning point in nature (as was traditional), he became the first artist of modern times to consider the appearance of his *pictorial form* more important than the *forms of nature,* themselves.

In this search for his own kind of "reality," he looked beneath the surface matter of the world for the universal or changeless form. He once wrote to a friend that he found all nature reducible to simple geometric shapes such as cones, spheres, and cubes. The essentialness of these forms seemed more permanent to Cézanne than the transient face of nature. Due to the intellectual processes involved in his "realizations" of form, he is considered a classicist in spirit; nevertheless he became the forerunner for modern Cubism as well as other intellectualized abstract forms of the twentieth century.

In contrast to the architectural character of Cézanne's forms, the work of Paul Gauguin shows the invention of a vivid, symbolic world of decorative patterns. They owe their particular character to the type of form expression found in medieval frescoes, mosaics, and enamels. Although his themes were inspired by the barbaric peoples of the South Seas, the works always demonstrate a sense of the sophistication typical of most western art. An underlying suavity tempers Gauguin's work and gives it a quality reminiscent of the old masters' paintings in spite of its barbarity of color and freedom of pattern. The decorative style of the French Fauves in the early twentieth century primarily stems from the work of Paul Gauguin.

The work of Vincent van Gogh, the third pioneer Post-Impressionist, represents the beginning of the new, highly-charged, *subjective expression* which we find in many forms of contemporary painting. The character of twentieth-century Expressionism owes a great deal to the impetuous brush strokes and the dramatic distortions of color and object forms first found in the work of Van Gogh.

Figure 135. PINES AND ROCKS by Paul Cézanne. Cézanne looked for the essential "essence" of natural forms rather than mere surface description. In this painting, the artist has simplified the tree and rock shapes to produce a solid compositional unity.

Courtesy The Museum of Modern Art, New York. Lillie P. Bliss Collection.

Twentieth-Century Forms of Expression

expressionism

French and German Expressionism, perhaps the most significant phase in the evolution of newer art forms, began as the first decade of the twentieth century was almost over. The young artists of this movement were the first to declare on a large scale the complete freedom of the artist to work in a manner consonant with his feeling about a subject. In a sense, we see these artists as merely being more liberal Romantics; however, it was possible to be more liberal only after those intervening years of change which had introduced new ways of "seeing" and "feeling."

The twentieth century saw the growth of a new awareness or consciousness which was related to the many changes taking place, or about to take place, in the whole order of existence. Cézanne, Gauguin, and Van Gogh had opened the door through which hosts of young artists were now eager to plunge; they were anxious to explore this new world of previously unknown artistic sensations, diversions, and mysteries. The shape of this new artistic world is signaled by an explosion of color and an exciting style of drawing which ran the gamut from the graceful curves of Matisse to the bold slashings of Kokoschka.

Colorplate 62

The Fauves. The members of the earliest Expressionist group were called the *Fauves.* This title was attached to them because of the "wild" appearance of their paintings in comparison to the academic formalism which was accepted and expected by the general public of the period. The term, literally translated, means "wild beasts." Where the public had been only dimly aware of Cézanne and Van Gogh as revolutionaries, they could not ignore this host of young painters which threw Paris into a turmoil with group exhibitions, pamphleteering, and other forms of personal publicity. In fact, the Fauves seemed to be trying to live up to the name which was attached to them; however, within a period of only seven years, they had lost their original vigor and

were accepted as rather calm compared to the newer movements which were evolving. Fauvism is a form of expression which tries to arrive at the emotional "essence" of a subject rather than its external appearance; its characteristic style is decorative, colorful, spontaneous, and intuitional. When the emotional excitement of the artist over his subject is communicated to the spectator, his work of art may be called successful.

The color, brilliance, and persuading sophistication found in the work of Henri Matisse, nominal leader of the group, was largely influenced by Persian and Near Eastern art. The group, as a whole, felt similar influences, often searching for "patterns" in the areas of the museums dedicated to older and more remote group expressions; they received inspiration from the work of the Byzantines, the Coptic Christians, the Greek artists of the archaic age, as well as the primitive tribal arts of Africa, Oceania, and the American Indian. The use of African masks and sculpture as sources of Matisse's style can be detected in the masklike, impersonal quality of the human faces found in his paintings. Back of this impersonal effect, there also seems to lie a sense of mystery or threat engendered by the enigmatic quality of an alien style of expression.

Despite the rather strong, vibrant color generally preferred by the Expressionists, Matisse, Utrillo, Derain, and Modigliani often build charming, decorative structures which continue the long tradition of classical restraint found in French and Italian art. Georges Roualt, on the other hand, is an exception in French Expressionism, his work being more dramatic like that of the Germans. His painting expresses a violent reaction to the hypocracy and materialism of his time through a favorite use of thick, crumbling reds and blacks. His images of Christ are symbols of man's inhumanity to man; his portrayal of judges reveals the crime and corruption that can reach even into those areas where justice should prevail. Roualt's comment, through his painting, on the French leaders of the day is anything but complimentary.

German Expressionism. Paralleling the movement in France, the artists of Germany felt that they, as prophets of new, unknown artistic values, must destroy the conventions which bound the art of their time. The foundation of painting in Europe for the next fifty years was provided in the aims of three groups of German artists: *Die Brucke* (The Bridge), the *Blaue Reiter* (Blue Knights), and *Die Neu Sachlichke*it (The New Objectivity). The Ex-

pressionism of these artists, drawn from an environment that seemed complacent toward social and political injustices, was ultimately an art of protest. While producing work which protested against the outrages of the period, the artists attempted to create in as direct a fashion as possible work which represented their basic urge for expression. The combination of this driving creative urge with the desire to protest became the foundation for a

Colorplates
63, 64, 65

Figure 136. ANXIETY by Edvard Munch. Some of the unhappy experiences in the life of this artist are presented with the characteristic exaggeration of emotional content. Childish terrors and medieval superstitions are interwoven into a form that is expressive of frightful conditions seen in our times.

Courtesy The Museum of Modern Art, New York.

number of varied movements in German art; the resulting art forms take on a quality of vehemence, drama, gruesomeness, and fanaticism never completely achieved through the *raison* (reason) of French art.

The young artists of this style identified themselves with the religious mysticism of the Middle Ages as well as the tribal arts of primitive peoples. Many followed the manner of children with their naive but direct expression of emotional identification with environment. For example, the art of Emil Nolde is similar in feeling to the mystic art of the Middle Ages while Edward Munch based many of his creations on medieval and primitive folk art traditions. Franz Marc was an artist who used

the emotional reality of caveman art as a basis for his inspiration. Protests against Prussian *jingoism* became the subject matter of the painting of George Grosz and Otto Dix. This characteristic aspect of Prussian culture led to the first World War and ultimately to Hitlerism and World War II.

Max Beckmann, although not a part of any organized group of Expressionists, followed a path somewhat kindred in spirit to the work of Otto Dix. Following World War I, Dix had worked in a style which satirized the swampy, degraded underworld of political society. Beckmann cultivated a similar style of frank, satirical veracity but modified his emotional intensity of expression with the calm, geometric arrange-

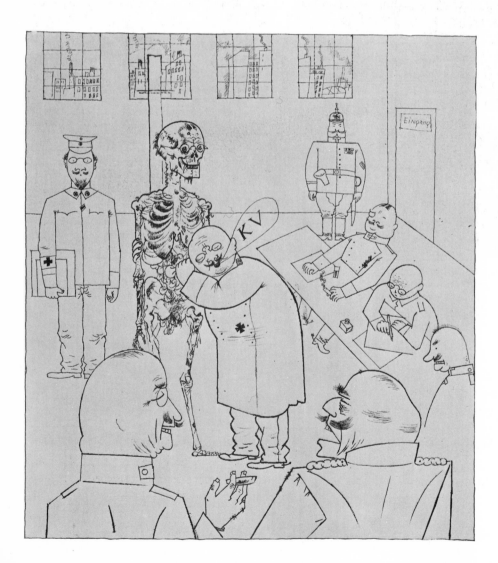

Figure 137. FIT FOR ACTIVE SERVICE by George Grosz. In this work, characteristic German emotionalism is forced to new limits of satire as a result of the artist's personal experiences during the First World War. Expressionism, which shows moral indignation at its peak, now becomes an instrument of social protest. Niceties of color are ignored in favor of harsh, biting black lines.

Courtesy The Museum of Modern Art, New York. A. Conger Goodyear Fund.

Figure 138. ELECTION NIGHT by Jack Levine. Influenced by the social and political problems of the post World War II period, the artist arrived at a distinctive manner which combines a complicated and glowing technique with an expressionist pungency of feeling.

Courtesy The Museum of Modern Art, New York. Gift of Joseph H. Hirshhorn.

ment which he had learned from Cubism. This latter quality gives a certainty of execution to his manner of painting quite reminiscent of the work of the "old masters."

Expressionism in United States and Mexico. The Expressionistic style had adherents in the Americas as well as in the European countries. The great depression of the "30's" influenced such artists as Max Weber and Ben Shahn to make mournful and satiric comment on Ameri-

can society of the period. Evergood and Levine are more recent artists who make similar commentary on the political and social confusion of the "cold war" years.

Mexico, during the "twenties" and "thirties," was undergoing an artistic renaissance which many artists found fruitful ground for an Expressionistic style—a style based on their identification of themselves with problems inherent in the growth of freedom for the Indian and mestizo classes. José Orozco, whose art evolved in this period, became the greatest exponent of Expressionism in the Western hemisphere. Inspired by the rapidly changing social order in Mexico, he produced work which has a quality of expression similar to that of Roualt in Europe. There is something of the same black tragedy in the work of both artists although, at the same time, each has a style different in form and meaning.

abstract art

Cubism—the beginning of Abstraction. Beginning about 1906 in Paris, a new attitude toward nature was observed in the work of certain artists. Before Cézanne, the artists of Europe tended to see nature in terms of material surfaces. Cézanne began the trend toward the search for "reality" (the universal unvariables) beneath these material surfaces by observing and emphasizing the basic structure

Figure 139. BARRICADE by José Clemente Orozco. Slashing diagonals of line combine with agitated hues and values to express the feeling of this artist concerning the furor of the Mexican social revolution in the early twentieth century.

Courtesy The Museum of Modern Art, New York.

Figure 140. MAN WITH VIOLIN, 1911 by Pablo Picasso. The shapes in Picasso's Facet-cubist style are component planes coaxed forth from subject forms and freely rearranged to suit the artist's design concepts. In some cases, the facets are retained in their original positions, and certain elements of the figure are fleetingly recognizable.

of nature. This new way of seeing developed gradually over a period of twenty-five years paralleling the changing concepts of "reality" in science. Cézanne had stated his concept that the artists should seek the universal forms of nature in the cube, the cone, and the sphere. Artistic explorations founded directly on this concept gradually developed in the work of the Fauves and finally resulted in a style labeled Cubism.

One of the most active young artists of the Fauve movement in Paris from 1903 to 1906 was the Spaniard, Pablo Picasso. Possibly because of his admiration for the work of Cézanne or because of a desire to challenge the leadership of the Fauves by Matisse, Picasso began to look for new possibilities of form expression in his painting. He based his explorations on an analysis of volume and space structure. With much of the same attitude as Cézanne, Picasso became dissatisfied with the emphasis on the external characteristics of objects and sought for a method of expressing their internal structure. He eventually developed paintings which displayed many facets of the same object at the same time on the same canvas. Many of Picasso's ideas may be traced back not only to Cézanne but to characteristic styles of primitive art forms—archaic Greek sculpture as well as African negro sculpture.

The most noticeable aspect of cubist form, as evolved by Picasso, his colleagues, and followers, was its geometric crystallization of shapes. By this means, the artists tried to arrive at a more permanent type of order than that found in natural form. At the same time, the traditional illusionistic rendering of space was reordered into what the artists felt was a more stable form of spatial relationship, independent of the vagaries of light and the distortions of shape caused by the use of linear perspective.

In his concern with arriving at a new statement of the structure of matter seen from an aesthetic point of view, Picasso often stripped away many aids to expression, for example, richness of color. However, in this process of reduction, he formulated a new artistic language that put an end to the respect for surface appearance observable in all art since the time of the Renaissance. Paintings were now made with the intention of primarily emphasizing the artistic devices *for their own sake* rather than merely adapting these devices to the *imitation of nature;* traditionally accepted object forms began to give way to "pure" or maximum form. With the new emphasis on the intrinsic quality of the artistic elements (line, shape, value, texture, and color) a new set of terms had to be invented in order to make a more convenient

Figure 141. MUSICAL FORMS, 1913 by Georges Braque. Braque varies the usually cubist handling of form by his inventive inclusion of textured foreign materials. Such textures added to the repertoire of contemporary art a new beauty of surface manipulation.

Courtesy Philadelphia Museum of Art. Louise and Walter Arensberg Collection.

explanation of what the artist was trying to do—especially for those who were not prepared to accept complete "purity" of form. The term, *abstraction,* which had had only a general meaning up to the 1900's, was now applied to this form of expression which was considered no longer associational with observed objects. Cubism, which is a semiabstract art form, can now be seen as the forerunner for all the later forms of *Abstraction* in art. In semiabstract art, we can generally still recognize certain objects from nature; the transformation of such forms in the process of abstraction is meant to express the artist's convictions about life and matter. Transformation of forms is a matter of degree and may vary from the semiabstract styles of Cubism and Futurism to the "pure" abstraction of Wassily Kandinsky and Piet Mondrian.

Cubism, as the beginning of abstract art, was of major importance. It was introduced to the world not only in the works of Picasso but also in those of George Braque, a French artist, who callaborated with him—the two artists occupy-

ing the same studio for a number of years. Braque added uniquely expressive quality to the usual cubist approach by the use of foreign textured materials which he attached to the canvas surface—such a use was termed *papier collé* or just *collage.* On the whole, he remained true to the typical French art tradition of quietness of expression in spite of his use of new forms; this was a contrast to the more forceful, explosive quality found in the work of Picasso. In all Braque's work during the peak years of cubist expression (1911 to 1914), there is a sense of charm in his restrained manipulation of color and value patterns; these patterns are developed in terms of the finite volume of space, one of the chief cubist idioms.

Two other cubists of note were Fernand Leger, another French artist, and Juan Gris, a fellow countryman of Picasso. These two preferred the more austere expression often found in Picasso, but not the violence which was the other side of that artist's personality. Leger and Gris developed individual form qualities

Figure 142. THE CITY, 1919 by Fernand Léger. The rigidity and simple geometric character of industrial structures were subjects ideally suited to the cubist style. The paintings of Léger follow this principle and become true products of a "machine-age aesthetic."

Courtesy Philadelphia Museum of Art, A. E. Gallatin Collection

within the cubist pattern which set them apart as important creators in their own right. Because of the impact of industry on society, Leger accepted the machine as a styling motif for cubist form. Instead of abstracting away from nature, Gris dealt with volumes or decorative patterns which suggested recognizable objects. He would then develop these shapes in the direction of object recognition without resort to mere imitation of superficial appearance.

Futurism—the second phase of Abstract art. Futurism, like Cubism, remained a submovement within the overall abstract category. Futurism was actually a form of Cubism remodelled by certain Italian artists who had been to Paris during the excitement caused by the new artistic ventures of Picasso and Braque. Among the more important artists in this movement were Umberto Boccioni and Giacomo Balla. These artists studied in France and on their return to Italy were much intrigued by the rapid advances that had been made in domestic industry. Together with the poet, Marino Marinetti, they formed a union of ideas. Their expression was formulated on the basis of the modern machine, the speed and violence of contemporary life, and the psychological effects of this ferment on human mentality and activity. Boccioni, Severini, and their followers attempted to show the beauty of modern machines through sheaves of lines and planes which created an effect of dynamic movement and tension within the canvas. The translation of rapid motion into artistic terms was a constant preoccupation. The Futurists also attempted to interpret contemporary incidents of violence such as riots, strikes, and war which presumably would affect future events.

Colorplate 66

The fervor of this group was not matched by its artistic contributions, as the artists merely energized the somewhat static geometry of Cubism and brought back richer coloring. Perhaps its attention to the new subject matter of the machine was the most important contribution, for other artists and the public became more aware of the nature of our times. Following the traditional mission of art this group expressed the age in which its art was created.

Pure Abstract art—the elimination of nature. During the period from 1910 to 1918, the idea of the complete elimination of nature from art became the chief motivation of artists throughout Europe. Deriving primarily from the experiments of Picasso, artists explored pure abstraction in two main directions. Some, like the Russian Wassily Kandinsky, preferred an emotional, sensuous expressionism which later influenced American abstract painting; other artists such as Mondrian were more interested in the cold precision of geometric arrangement. Kandinsky's best known work featured powerful rhythms and loose biomorphic shapes which have a feeling of great spontaneity. Although it was rarely evident, Kandinsky's paintings usually originated with specific conditions or circumstances of some kind. The artist always attempted an interpretation of his responses to these in terms of pure visual language without reference to their outward appearance. Kandinsky's loose, direct manner is essentially that of a romantic; his appeal is directed at pure emotion, and in order to assess his works, the observer must have an experience similar to that which motivated the artist. Later, while working at the German Bauhaus (an architectural school which stressed the unity of all art in terms of design), Kandinsky's work began to show the influence of the geometric abstraction practiced by some of its artists.

The most representative exponent of geometric abstraction was Piet Mondrian of Holland. Like Kandinsky, Mondrian dealt with the pure elements of form, but, unlike Kandinsky, purged them of the emotional extremes of romanticism. Mondrian's art is the unemotional rationalization of line, shape, value, and color pushed to maximum optical purity. In such work, the meaning or content is inherent in the precise relationships established. This direction seemed sterile and shallow to artists and critics alike when it first appeared; that it was, instead, momentous and rich in possibilities seems proven by the tremendous impact it had on thousands of artists. The dissidents who had taken verbal slaps at geometric abstraction were soon in the minority.

Colorplate 62. INTERIOR WITH A VIOLIN CASE by Henri Matisse. Like the other Fauves, Matisse does not describe objects so much as he projects through his painting an emotional identification with those objects. The resulting painting shows a typically French sense of charm and orderliness despite the apparent freedom of drawing and color.

Collection The Museum of Modern Art, New York. Lillie P. Bliss Collection.

Colorplate 63. GYPSY WOMAN WITH BABY by Amedeo Modigliani. The artist's painting stresses sensitive shape arrangement and subtle modeling of form within a shallow space concept. His interpretation of the figure is a personal mannerism suggesting the influence of Gothic and African negro sculpture.

Courtesy The National Gallery of Art, Washington, D.C. Chester Dale Collection.

Colorplate 64. THE THREE JUDGES by Georges Rouault. The Expressionist's intensity of feeling is accomplished in terms of color by the use of somber reds framed in black and nocturnal blue. Rouault's work lacks the ingratiating character usually found in that of the other French artists of the movement.

Courtesy The Museum of Modern Art, New York. Sam A. Lewisohn Bequest.

Colorplate 65. DEPARTURE by Max Beckmann. Here style is emotionally intensified through strong contrasts of value and the impasto with which the artist has applied his pigment. However, this intensity of expression is partially modified by the cool, orderly arrangement derived from Cubism.

Courtesy The Museum of Modern Art, New York.

Colorplate 66. SPEEDING AUTOMOBILE, 1912 by Giacomo Balla. This artist's handling of the image of a speeding machine is characteristic of the Futurist idiom. Incorporated into the dynamic form is a sense of the hysterical approach to violence and the psychological impact of tensions in modern times.

Collection The Museum of Modern Art, New York.

Colorplate 67. NO. 10 by Mark Rothko. Using apparent simple masses of color on a large scale, the artist is able to evoke emotional sensations in the observer. Mark Rothko is one of the younger generation of American artists who work in the Pure Abstract idiom.

Collection The Museum of Modern Art, New York. Gift of Philip C. Johnson.

Colorplate 68. VILLAGE IN THE FIELDS by Paul Klee. Many artists developed fusions of twentieth-century concepts which defy classification insofar as any one category of expression is concerned. This reproduction illustrates a refined synthesis of relaxed Cubistic forms and the naive charm of children's art.

Collection The Museum of Modern Art, New York. Katherine S. Dreier Bequest.

Colorplate 69. PERSON THROWING A STONE AT A BIRD by Joan Miro. In this painting, Miro shows sophisticated color and bio-morphic shapes combined with simple child-like images. In many respects, it is similar to the Klee painting illustrated earlier in the book. The Abstract Surrealism of Miro is, in general, semi-representational in character.

Courtesy The Museum of Modern Art, New York.

Colorplate 70. WOMAN, I by Willem de Kooning. The artist summarizes most aspects of the "Romantic" or "Action" group of abstract expressionism: revelation of the ego through the act of painting, neglect of academic or formal organization in favor of bold, direct, free gestures that are instinctively organized, and willingness to explore unknown and undescribable effects and experiences. Even though he seems to use the figure, its representational value is subordinated by the motivating "activity" of pure painting.

Courtesy The Museum of Modern Art, New York.

Colorplate 71. DOUBLE METAMORPHOSIS II by Agam (Yaacov Gipstein). The "Op" Artist explores not only the psychology of sight but the physical effect which viewing his forms of art may generate. In some ways, the forms of "Op" Art seem an extension of earlier twentieth - century geometric abstract art.

Collection The Museum of Modern Art, New York. Gift of Mr. and Mrs. George Jaffin.

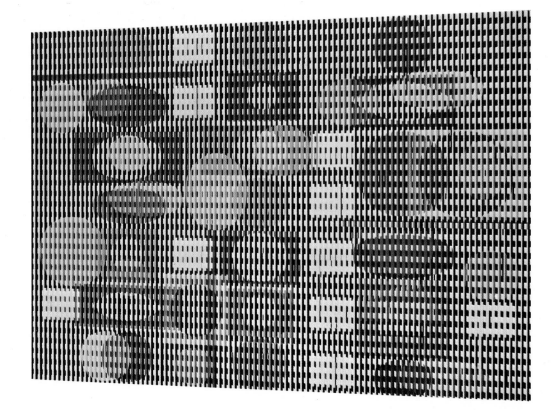

Figure 143. IMPROVISATION No. 30 by Wassily Kandinsky. About 1910, the Russian, Wassily Kandinsky, began to paint freely moving, biomorphic shapes in rich combinations of hues. The characteristic early style which the artist evolved may be seen in this illustration. Such an abstract form of expression was an attempt to show the artist's feelings about object surfaces rather than to describe their outward appearances.

Courtesy The Art Institute of Chicago.

Figure 144. COMPOSI-
TION IN WHITE, BLACK,
AND RED, by Piet Mon-
drian. Mondrian created
a "pure" art purged of all
but the elements of art
structure. His simple, bold
style, evolved from a study
of the subtle relationships
of these elements has
been readily assimilated
into many forms of con-
temporary expression. Its
influence on commercial
and industrial design of
today is quite obvious.

Courtesy The Museum of Modern Art, New York. Gift of the
Advisory Committee.

Colorplate
67

nonobjective variants of abstract art

Heretofore, the abstract art discussed has originated with nature; the next development was so-called Nonobjective painting which presumed to divorce itself from nature altogether and originate entirely (insofar as this can be determined) within the mind of the artist. The differences in Pure-Abstraction and Nonobjective works of art are not readily apparent; perhaps attempts to differentiate are only of theoretical interest. Both concepts opened up a new realm of aesthetic endeavor, and explorations in this area continue down to the present time. Obviously, the term "Nonobjective" is not to be interpreted as meaning that the artist has no objective; the artist is very definitely attempting to communicate but without resort to *objective* reporting. A certain amount of pure abstract and nonobjective work is more imita-

tive than original. Synthetic abstraction is easily produced as an end in itself. However, it is as a creative process that abstraction is more properly employed and this calls for the maximum powers of the artist.

A great part of what we see in our world today has been given its personality by the continuing influence of the abstract concept. The theories of form underlying this concept were readily assimilated by modern design. Buildings, furniture, textiles, advertising layout, machines, and costume are only a few of the areas which bear witness to the tremendous impact of abstract art. Stylistically, the gap has constantly narrowed between "fine" art and art of a commercial or industrial nature. This may be, in part, due to the fact that abstract art developed out of an environment in which the practical function of the machine

Figure 145. BRIDGE V, 1919 by Lyonel Feininger. American artists inheriting a tradition of native romantic realism seemed to have been reluctant to accept pure abstract expression. Inspired by the dramatic shapes found in man-made structures, but informed by the careful designs of cubism, Feininger eventually merges these two forms of expression in a semi-abstract style.

Courtesy Philadelphia Museum of Art.

had become an unconscious as well as a conscious part of life. In a sense the abstract artist created a "machine-age" aesthetic.

abstract art in the united states

Abstract art was slow in coming to America, but shortly after the second World War, it quickly gathered momentum. The influence of European expatriate artists was an important factor in this change. Actually, many American artists, during the period between the two world wars, had been affected by the structural order of Cubism. John Marin, Lyonel Feininger, Georgia O'Keefe, Stuart Davis, and Marsden Hartley were among the early pioneers of abstraction on these shores. In a peculiarly American way, however, they seem to have refrained from going completely over to pure abstraction and retained a strongly personalized vision. After World War II, a new generation of younger American artists renounced the last ties with nature. Some of the leaders in this movement of the mid-1940's were Irene Rice Pereira and Loren MacIver among the women, and G.L.K. Morris (who actually began pure abstraction in the thirties), Bradley

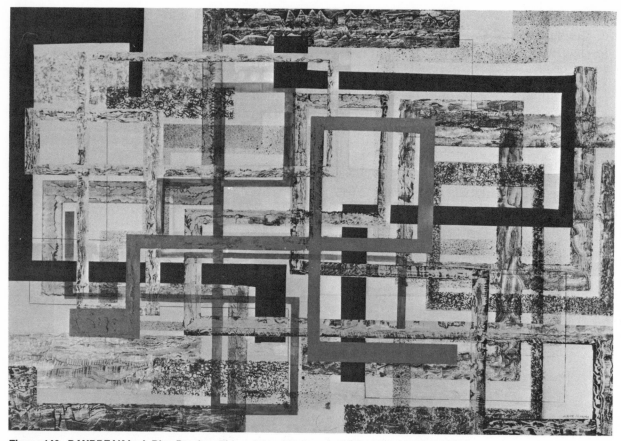

Figure 146. DAYBREAK by I. Rice Pereira. This painter developed a style of abstraction which investigates space, light, and dimensions; all of which are inherent in the structure of the painting itself. Her work is one of the unique variations that the general concept of abstraction has taken in this country.

Courtesy The Metropolitan Museum of Art. Gift of Edward J. Gallagher, Jr., 1955. The Edward Joseph Gallagher III Collection.

Walker Tomlin, and Mark Rothko among the men. Toward the end of the "40's," a new impulse, stemming from a mixture of abstraction, surrealism, and expressionism, began to be manifest. Pure geometric abstraction began to slip almost indistinguishably over into this new direction. We must now go back in time to see how this came about.

fantastic art: background of fantasy and dadaism

A third major direction in twentieth-century art began to be recognizable about 1914, the first year of World War I. The war had evidently begun to raise questions about the individual's ability to master the machine; this suggested that individual freedoms might actu-

ally be destroyed in this age of technology. As a kind of antidote to the machine cult in abstract art, certain writers, poets, and artists began to extol artistic forms which reemphasized the emotional, subconscious side of creativity. During the period, for instance, Picasso's art went away from the ennobled, monumental structures of early Cubism and began to take on structural perversions which eventually were to be the basis for Dadaism's destructive, cynical, and absurd puns on the cult of materialism in society.

A certain element of artistic endeavor in the past had been devoted to the creative invention of images that seemed manifestations of weird and fantastic imaginations. The centaurs of the Greeks; the strange beast-symbols of human sin in medieval manuscripts and sculpture; the superstitions, alchemist's nightmares of Jerome Bosch in the early sixteenth century; and the fantasies of Goya in the late eighteenth and early nineteenth centuries may be cited as a few of the prototypes for twentieth-century fantasy.

The years of the first World War nurtured the growth of an art that emphasized the irrational side of human behavior. Neutral Switzerland had become the mecca for poets, writers, artists, liberals, and political exiles who had sought refuge there from persecution or the terrors of modern warfare. Out of the intellectual ferment largely motivated by disillusionment arose "Dada," a semiphilosophic creed for the protestation of the moral and social degeneracy which, it was felt, was responsible for the war. According to Dada, a complete erasure of

accepted institutions and conventions was needed; only on completely virgin soil could mankind rebuild a more desirable society. The Dadaists, therefore, embarked on a programmatic undermining of traditional "civilized" mores by cynical and sardonic derision of all its manifestations.

Duchamp, Picabia, Ernst, and others began to fashion machinelike humanized forms which suggested the robotizing of man. Later, with even more remarkable ingenuity, they created biomorphic images which discredited the semiorganic qualities of Kandinsky's romanticised abstract art. These inventions were meant to show disrespect for the experimental forms of the art leaders of the early century and shock a public already disturbed by a visual revolution.

The basic premise of this bizarre movement was that every Dadaist was given complete

Figure 147. THE HORSE, HE'S SICK, 1920 by Max Ernst. As a part of the Dadaist' debunking of all twentieth century art forms, a natural organism is here turned into a mechanical absurdity. At the same time, the use of pasted photo-engravings is a nonsensical twist of the collage technique first invented by the cubist, Braque.

Courtesy The Museum of Modern Art, New York.

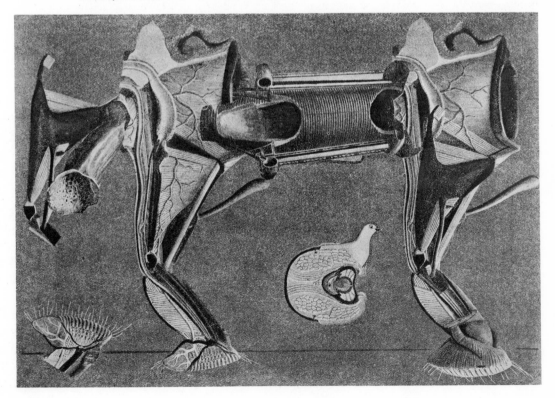

expressive freedom in his attack on the old order. In principle, there was no limit to the disorder which might be projected in painting, poetry, or general social behavior. All of this left a bad taste in the mouth of the general layman, and he usually classifies all of modern art with the outlandish forms executed by the Dadaists. Actually, its disorder eventually led to the demise of the movement. Dada was pure negativism, an exhibitionism of the absurd; being against art, its only medium was nonsense publicly displayed to discredit all forms of sense. Its main value today is a historical one as the principal source of Surrealism and the liberator of expressive freedom.

individual fantasists

The inclination toward private fantasy seemed to be a general tendency in Western Europe during the period of Dada satire. This fantasy took individual, but quite influential directions in the hands of certain artists who were not a part of the Dada movement. Giorgio de Chirico, an Italian, placed incongruous modern machines in ancient shadowed plazas. The decadence of the modern world seems implied by the image of a classical world of silent squares inhabited by statue-like remnants of an unknown people. The frozen, unprogressive, and even trance-like expression seems to suggest a wistful desire to recover the past.

Figure 148. THE SOOTHSAYER'S RECOMPENSE, 1913 by Giorgio de Chirico. This picture combines with poetic fullness symbols of the past (classical statue and the Renaissance architecture) with forms of the modern world (railroad train) to create a vast feeling of a timeless and universal scene. In this way, de Chirico was able to emphasize the "reality of a personal symbolism."

Courtesy Philadelphia Museum of Art. Louise and Walter Arensberg Collection.

better acquaintance, his underlying humanitarianism is revealed.

surrealism

Figure 149. I AND THE VILLAGE, 1911 by Marc Chagall. The fairy-tale world of the imagination is found in this example by another artist who evades fixed classification. Recent technological concepts are reflected in the freely interpreted transparency of object forms and the disregard of gravity.

Courtesy The Museum of Modern Art, New York. Mrs. Simon Guggenheim Fund.

Paul Klee, a Swiss, created an art of witty, abstract imagery which was based on Expressionism and Cubism. His work seems to poke gentle, but penetrating fun at the cult of the machine and smile shyly at human pretensions. There seems to be the implication that there is more to extra-sensorial perception than modern man's addiction to practicality will allow.

Marc Chagall, Russian born but a resident of France and the United States, originally worked in an Expressionist manner. His stay in France brought him under the discipline of Cubism. Eventually, he joined the two styles in his own brand of romanticised, poetic art which has an "Alice in Wonderland" quality. Chagall freely X-rays people and floats them about in a gravity-free world. The first contact with Chagall usually brings a chuckle to the spectator. On

Surrealism was brought into being about 1924 out of the work of the individual fantasists and Dadaists. With the war over, there was once again a semblance of stability and a tendency for the public to become complacent about the ills of modern society. The Surrealists reacted to this by attempting to reassert "the importance of the individual's psychic life, and intended to preserve the life of the imagination against the threatening pressures and tensions of the contemporary world."[3]

According to Dr. Lester Longman, "Surrealism was Dada reborn with a program."[4] Both were a continuation of the counterattack (first instigated by the Romantics of the nineteenth century) against mechanistic materialism. The Romantics often created the hallucinatory imagery in which the Surrealist delights. In so doing, they gave evidence of the growing belief that man could not solve every problem by the right application of science and that little-known, often seemingly unsolvable problems, existed within the human mind. Sigmund Freud's theories of dreams and their meanings lent strong credence to this belief. Operating on this thesis, Surrealist artists created a new pantheon of subconscious imagery which was claimed to be more "real" than activities and behaviour on the conscious level. The surrealists believed that only in dreams, which arise from the mind below the conscious level, (nightmares or daydreams) had man retained his personal liberties. In their art, the Surrealists cultivated images which arise unbidden from the mind. These were recorded through "automatic" techniques of drawing and painting. Such images bring to attention the heretofore unrecognized arbitrariness of our senses concerning reality by exploring incongruous relationships of normal objects in abnormal settings. Common sense

Colorplate
68

---

[3]McCurdy, Charles, editor, *Modern Art: A Pictorial Anthology*, Macmillian Co., New York, 1958, p. 40-41.
[4]Longman, Lester, Notes from Longman's Lectures on Modern Art.

notions of space, time, and scale were juxtaposed in unfamiliar ways by the Surrealists.

Max Ernst's "frottages" (invented about 1925) was one technique used by the Surrealists to shut off the conscious mind. These were rubbings made on rough surfaces with crayon, pencil, or similar media. In the resulting impressions, the artist would search for a variety of incarnations while in a state of feverish mental intoxication. A process that borders on self-hypnosis was practiced to arrive at this state. Some artists, such as Salvador Dali, effected a similar creative fever, but used a meticulous, naturalistic technique to give authenticity to his improbable, weird, and shocking images. Yves Tanguy used a method similar to Ernst's. Allowing his hand to wander in free and unconscious "doodlings," he used his creative visualization to bring on nonfigurative objects which suggested life. Tanguy's pictorial shapes have the appearance of sentient, alien organisms which live in a mystical twilight land.

There have been many Surrealist artists, but Ernst, Dali, and Tanguy have been most influential, thanks to their unflagging invention of arresting images. The influence of these outstanding artists extended to the great number of other artists who did not hold to the restrictions of the Orthodox Surrealist brotherhood as set forth in Andre Breton's manifesto of 1924. Many of these artists used some of the methods of the group while designing in a formal manner (an approach disdained by Orthodox Surrealists) thus combining the methods of the Abstractionists, the Surrealists, and the Expressionists.

Figure 150. THE PERSISTENCE OF MEMORY, 1931 by Salvador Dali. Here we find a naturalistic technique of representation to give authenticity to improbable Surrealist images. Dali bends watches as if they were made of a soft, rubbery substance and otherwise adjusts natural objects to suit the fantastic world of his imagination.

Courtesy The Museum of Modern Art, New York.

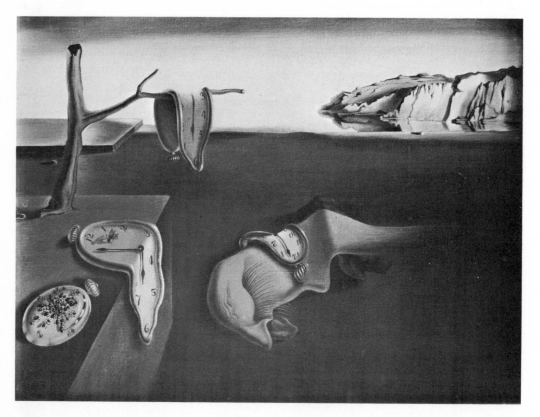

Figure 151. MULTIPLICATION DES ARCS, 1954 by Yves Tanguy. Commonly working with nonfigurative objects in a polished technique, the Surrealist, Tanguy invents a new world that gives the appearance of being peopled by lifelike gems.

Abstract Surrealism

Since about 1925 there have been a host of artists who mix certain aspects of the three major directions of early twentieth-century art. Generally speaking, these artists found pure abstraction too impersonal, machinelike and dehumanized. On the other hand, Surrealism seemed to disregard a desire for order that has traditionally been held fundamental to art.

Among the artists who chose a harmony of shape relationships stemming from Abstraction mixed with Surrealism's unbidden imagery are: Joan Miró of Spain, Rufino Tamayo of Mexico, Matta Echaurren of Chile, Mark Tobey of the United States, and some ex-Europeans, such as Willem de Kooning, Arshile Gorky and Hans

Colorplate
69

Hoffman. These latter three artists, who lived in the United States after World War II (some came to the U.S. in the decade previous, others during the war), helped pioneer the first American art movement called Abstract Expressionism.

Abstract Expressionism

As a movement, Abstract Expressionism came about in the late 1940's. It is divided into two basic groups: a generally romantic direction (often called "action painting"), and a more classical group closely allied to the geometric branch of pre-World War II Abstraction. In the first group were such artists as Jackson Pollock, Franz Kline and Clifford Still. These artists

Figure 152. AGONY, 1947, by Arshile Gorky.
An engineering, as well as artistic background, in Gorky's student days, plus the stimulation of Surrealism's unbidden imagery led this artist into the emotionalized phase of Abstract Expressionism. There is a peculiar quality in his work of precision and stability becoming unsettled and unsettling that marks a personal life of inevitable change and tragedy. Gorky was an important influence on the younger generation of American Abstract Expressionists in the 1940's.

Courtesy, The Museum of Modern Art, New York, A. Conger Goodyear Fund.

Figure 153. THREADING LIGHT, 1942, by Mark Tobey.
Tobey was not directly a member of the small group of young Americans who originally founded the Abstract Expressionist movement in the immediate post World War II years, but seems to be formally related. He originated his own personal method of linear expression in painting (called "white writing") which causes accretions of line to waver on the edge of shape recognition only to slip off into an abstract controlled-tension between surface and space.

Courtesy, The Museum of Modern Art, New York.

turned to an artistic manner that reminds one of the emotional content of the early Kandinsky's (before 1921). Some acknowledge that even so unlikely a source as Monet suggested a kindred technical method. Confusion, fear, and uncertainty about man's place in a world threatened by thermonuclear holocaust may have led others to reject most of the forms of previous twentieth-century art and, as a kind of personal catharsis, to express their belief in the "value of doing" at the expense of disciplined design. Thus, Jackson Pollock, frequently cited as the chief exponent of the "Action" painting trend in Abstract Expressionism, created swirling images of a nonrepresentational kind out of linear skeins of fast-drying paint dripped directly onto large canvases, expressing the reality of self in the act of creation.

Franz Kline, another member of the "Action group," took a slightly different direction, but with similar intentions of expressing the self through direct contact with the forms created. He utilized drawings made with gestures of a brush on newsprint, which were cut up and reassembled to provide a sense of power and intensified personal rapport. Kline utilized these "sketches" as guides to their enlargement on big canvases without actually copying them. House painters' brushes and savage slashings in black and white, or sometimes in color, became monumental projections of inward experiences. A similar kind of daring and willingness to explore the unknown, which such artists displayed in revealing their ego, is expected of the viewer to renew the experience of creativity. This conscious attempt to involve the spectator in art is, perhaps, the leit motif of directions in the second half of this century. This involvement of the viewer has gone far beyond a similar endeavour attempted in seventeenth-century European religious art. Perhaps the reason may be that artists foresee that as urban sprawl causes man to want to isolate himself from its pressures and tensions; involvement in art has to be forced on the spectator, somewhat like a tonic, for his own good.

The second branch of artists, within Abstract Expressionism, given to a more restrained manner allied to the geometric branch of pre-war Abstraction, includes Mark Rothko, Carl Holty, Ad Reinhardt, and Robert Motherwell, to name a few. Many of these artists were motivated by the subtle color relationships of Joseph Albers, a former teacher at the German Bauhaus and emigree to the United States during World War II. Hans Hoffman was another influence on them. All these artists appear concerned with reducing form to the sensation of color or value alone. They tend to create broad areas of color or of shapes so closely related in value and/or color that they are not immediately detectable. Both types of painting seem to enwrap the spectator and make them a part of the

Figure 154. NUMBER 1, Jackson Pollock.
This artist is considered the prime example among the youthful exponents of Abstract Expressionist "action painting" in the late 1940's. He is primarily noted for the creation of swirling non-representational images in linear-skeins of fast drying paint which he applied by dripping directly onto canvases through controlled gestures of his tools.

Courtesy, The Museum of Modern Art, New York.

painting as an experienced sensation. The intention seems akin in final analysis to the "Action" painter group discussed previously, but their paintings are not violent recollections of the emotional fervor of painting, rather they are quiet insinuations on the viewer's being.

Pop and Op Art

Since the early 1960's, the dominance of Abstract Expressionism has been challenged by two main variations of international trends called "Pop" and "Op" art. The term "Pop," stands for Popular Art, or even for "Pop Bottle" Art; judging by the frequency with which such objects have appeared. The movement as a whole seems to have originated in England in the fifties and then became rather naturally ac-

climated to the United States. In it, images made popular by mass media advertising, comic strips, and other objects of everyday association, such as pop bottles, beer cans, or super market products are presented in bizarre combinations, distortions or exaggerations of size, but always rendered with fidelity to the original man-made objects. The effect of these objects, as in the case of Andrew Warhol's *Campbell Soup Cans*, or Roy Lichtenstein's grotesquely magnified comic strip heroes and villains, is to cause the viewer to react in a manner best described by the slang expression "double take." As with Abstract Expressionism, the observer is again involved directly in the work of art, but now it is by the frequency with which he sees these commonplace items in everyday life

Colorplate
70

Figure 155. THE AMERICAN DREAM I by Robert Indiana. This is an example of "Pop" Art. Robert Indiana utilizes the "Pop" convention of commonly seen images of advertising. He mixes it with slogan conscious idioms of daily American life to create new experiences in which the conventional becomes unconventional.

Courtesy The Museum of Modern Art, New York.

and not alone as an experienced sensation of the art form itself. There is a blurring that takes place between the realm of art and real life in Pop Art which has become increasingly pronounced in the more recent, Pop originated, "Happenings."

Since similar experiences were promoted by the Dadaists in 1916, Pop artists are sometimes called "Neo-Dadaists." But whereas Dada was nihilistic, self-exterminating and satirical, Pop Art seems to have little of such purposes. Instead, there is a more joyful enthusiasm for exploring the possibilities which the daily images and objects of megalo metropolitan society and culture seem to imply. Significant artists of Pop persuasion who might be included, besides Warhol and Lichtenstein, are: Jime Dine, Robert Indiana, Tom Wesselman, Robert Rauschenberg, Claes Oldenburg, and George Segal. Several of these, but especially Oldenburg and Segal, are sculptors or assemblers; in which fields Pop art makes inroads as much as in painting.

"Op" Art stands for the term, Optical. This trend seems merely an extension and modification again of earlier twentieth-century Geometric Abstraction and Non-objectivity. Artists in the movement (many again influenced by Albers), such as Victor Vasarely, Richard Anuskiewicks, George Ortman and Bridget Riley, employ precise shapes and sometimes wriggly lines or concentric patterns that have a direct impact on the physiology and psychology of sight. They have explored moiré patterns and have formed groups which seem almost more dedicated to the scientific investigation of vision than to its intuitive expression in art.

Thus, new and vital forms of expression keep emerging from the fusion of fundamental twentieth-century manners. With so much emphasis today on the "new" for its own sake, it does not seem surprising that there is little resistance to almost anything displayed as art, but the significance of these new forms, according to the critic Harold Rosenberg, can be determined by their relevance to our time and place, just as significant movements in art have been for centuries.

Figure 156. CUT MERINGUES by Wayne Thiebaud. This artist, like Warhol and many other "Pop" artists, takes objects of everyday associations out of their normal visual context. By bringing particularized pictorial or sculptural attention to these objects, rather than the normal centralized scanning they receive, the artist makes the observer aware of new visual values that can be found in mundane forms.

Courtesy The Museum of Modern Art, New York.

APPENDIX I: GLOSSARY OF TERMS

Abstract, abstraction. A term given to forms created by the artist but usually derived from objects actually observed or experienced. It usually involves a simplification and/or rearrangement of natural objects to meet the needs of artistic organization or expression. Sometimes there is so little resemblance to the original object that the shapes seem to have no relationship to anything ever experienced in our natural environment.

Academic. A term applied to any kind of art which stresses the use of accepted rules for technique and form organization. It represents the exact opposite of the original approach which results in a vital, individual style of expression.

Accent. Any stress or emphasis given to elements of a composition which makes them attract more attention than other features which surround or are close to them. Accent may be created by brighter color, darker tone, greater size, or any other means by which difference may be expressed.

Achromatic. Relating to differences of lightness and darkness; the absence of color.

Aesthetics. The theory of the artistic or the "beautiful"; traditionally a branch of philosophy, but now a compound of the philosophy, psychology, and sociology of art. As a compound of the above, aesthetics is no longer solely confined to determining what is beautiful in art, but now attempts to discover the origins of sensitivity to art forms, and the relationships of art to other phases of culture (such as science, industry, morality, philosophy, and religion).
Frequently used in this book to mean concern with artistic qualities of form as opposed to descriptive form or a mere recording of facts in visual form (see Objective).

Amorphous. Without clarity of definition; formless; indistinct and of uncertain dimensions.

Analagous Colors. (1) Closely related colors, especially those in which we can see one common hue. (2) Colors which are neighboring on the color wheel.

Approximate symmetry. The use of forms which are similar on either side of a vertical axis. They may give a feeling of the exactness of equal relationship but are sufficiently varied to prevent visual monotony.

Artificial Texture. Textures of products created by man; i.e., glass, steel, plastic, etc.

Asymetrical balance. A form of balance attained when the visual units on either side of a vertical axis are not identical but are placed in positions within the pictorial field so as to create a "felt" equilibrium of the total form concept.

Balance. A feeling of equality in weight, attention, or attraction of the various visual elements within the pictorial field as a means of accomplishing organic unity.

Biomorphic shapes. Shapes which are irregular in form and resemble the freely developed curves found in organic life.

Calligraphy. The use of flowing rhythmical lines which intrigue the eye as they enrich surfaces. Calligraphy is highly personal in nature similar to the individual qualities found in hand-writing.

Chiaroscuro. A technique of representation which concentrates on the effects of blending the light and shade on objects to create the illusion of space or atmosphere.

Chromatic. Relating to color.

Classical. Art forms which are characterized by a rational, controlled, clear, and intellectual approach. The term derives from the ancient art of Greece in the 4th and 5th centuries B.C. The term *classic* has an even more general connotation, meaning an example or model of first rank or highest class for any kind of form, literary, artistic, natural or otherwise. *Classicism* is the application or adherence to the principles of Greek culture by later cultural systems such as Roman classicism, Renaissance classicism, or the art of the Neo-Classic movement of the early 19th century (see Chapter 10, Forms of Expression).

Collage. Similar to papier collé except that materials of all kinds are admissible to the picture. Painted and drawn passages are combined with scrap materials to create the desired effects.

Color. The character of surface created by the response of vision to the wavelength of light reflections.

Color Triad. A group of three colors spaced an equal distance apart on the color wheel. There is a primary triad, a secondary triad, and two intermediate triads on the twelve-color wheel.

Complementary Colors. Two colors which are directly opposite each other on the color wheel. A primary color would be complementary to a secondary color which was a mixture of the two remaining primaries.

Composition. The act of organizing all of the elements of a work of art into a harmoniously unified whole. Each element used may have intrinsic characteristics which create interest, but it must function in such a way that "the whole is more important than its parts."

Concept. A comprehensive idea or generalization which brings diverse elements into some basic relationship.

Content (meaning). The essential meaning, significance, or aesthetic value of an art form. The psychological or sensory properties one tends to "feel" in art forms as opposed to the visual aspects of a work of art.

Contour. A line which creates a boundary separating an area of space from its surrounding background.

Craftsmanship. Aptitude, skill, or manual dexterity in the use of tools and materials.

Cubism. A term given to the artistic style which uses mostly geometric shapes usually two-dimensional in nature.

Curvilinear. Stressing the use of curved lines as opposed to *rectilinear* which stresses straight lines.

Dadaism. A nihilistic, anti-art, anti-everything movement resulting from the social, political, and psychological dislocations of World War I. The movement is important historically as a generating force for surrealism.

Decorative. The quality which emphasizes the two-dimensional nature of any of the visual elements. Decoration enriches a surface without denying the essential flatness of its nature.

Decorative shapes. Two-dimensional shapes which seem to lie next to each other on a picture surface; shapes which divide or break up the pictorial surface into smaller areas.

Decorative Space. A concept in which the visual elements have interval relationships in terms of a two-dimensional plane.

Decorative value. A type of pattern dependent more on the standard or local value of shapes rather than the representation of light and shadow; essentially a two-dimensional use of pattern.

Descriptive art. A manner or attitude based upon adherence to visual appearances.

Design. A framework or scheme of pictorial construction on which the artist bases the formal organization of his total work. In a broader sense, it may be considered as synonymous with the term, *form.*

Distortion. Any change made by an artist in the size, position or general character of forms based on visual perception, when those forms are organized into a pictorial image. Any personal or subjective interpretation of natural forms must necessarily involve a degree of distortion.

Dominance. The principle of visual organization which suggests that certain elements should assume more importance than others in the same composition. It contributes to organic unity by emphasizing the fact that there is one main feature and that other elements are subordinate to it.

Elements of art structure. The basic visual signs as they are combined into optical units which are used by the artist to communicate or express his creative ideas. The combination of the basic elements of line, shape, value, texture, and color represent the visual language of the artist.

Expression. A general term meaning the special characteristics of form which mark the work of an artist or group of artists. The "style" or "manner" in which artists attempt to say something about their times in terms of the artistic forms then considered to be of aesthetic merit.

When a work of art remains largely realistic in form but strongly emotional or intellectual in content, we call the work of art *expressive.* In a more general usage of the term, all art can be so characterized when the final goal is an intrinsic or self-sufficient aesthetic meaning. Opposed to this would be art with extrinsic, practical ends; commercial art, with its easily read message, is intended to promote a product other than a work of art itself.

Expressionistic art is art in which there is a desire to express what is "felt" rather than perceived or reasoned. Expressionistic form is defined by an obvious exaggeration of natural objects for the purpose of emphasizing an emotion, mood, or concept. It may be better understood as a more vehement kind of *romanticism.* The term *expressionism* is best applied to a movement in art of the early 20th century, although it may be used to describe all art of this character.

Fantasy (in art). Departure from accepted appearances or relationships for the sake of psychological expression—may exist within any art style, but usually thought of in connection with realism; unencumbered flights of pictorial fancy, freely interpreted or invented.

Fauvism. A name (meaning "wild beasts") for an art movement that began in Paris about 1905. It is expressionist art in a general sense but more decorative and with more of a French sense of orderliness and charm than is found in German expressionism (see Chapter 10, "Forms of Expression").

Form. The arbitrary organization or inventive arrangement of all of the visual elements according to principles which will develop an organic unity in the total work of art.

Form-meaning. Another term for *Content*, the third component of a work of art as used in this book. Since artists create artistic forms which cause spectator reactions, form-meaning implies that such reactions are the associations and/or sensory experiences which the observer finds in those forms.

Formal. An orderly system of organization as opposed to a less disciplined system.

Futurism. A sub-movement within the framework of abstract directions taken by many 20th century artists. The expression of futurist artists was based on an interest in time and rhythm which they felt were manifested in the machinery and human activities of modern times.

Genre. Painting stressing subject matter of domestic trivia, homey scenes, sentimental family life, etc.

Geometric shapes. Those shapes created by the exact mathematical laws of geometry. They are usually simple in character such as the triangle, the rectangle, the circle.

Graphic. As used in this book, the term refers to forms *physically* existing in a two-dimensional space relationship. For example, the graphic arts would refer only to those arts whose elements are present on a two-dimensional surface although they might give the *illusion* of three-dimensional quality.

Harmony. The unity of all of the visual elements of a composition achieved by the repetition of the same characteristics or those which are similar in nature.

Highlight. The area of a form which receives *directly* the greatest amount of light falling on it.

Hue. This designates the common name of a color and indicates its position in the spectrum or in the color circle. Hue is determined by the specific wavelength of the color in the ray of light.

Illusionism. The imitation of visual reality created on the flat surface of the picture plane by the use of perspective, light-and-dark shading, etc.

Illustration(al). An art practice, usually commercial in character, which stresses anecdote or story, situation, and subject in preference to serious considerations of aesthetic quality; non-eloquent, non-formal, easily understood, and temporal rather sustained or universal.

Image. An arresting aspect; a mentally envisioned thing or plan given concrete appearance through the use of an art medium; the general appearance of a work (en toto).

Impression, and Impressionism. A strong immediate effect produced in the mind by an outward or inward agency. Artists may work in this general sense (as Impressionists) at any time in history. The specific movement known as *Impressionism* was a late 19th century movement, primarily connected with painters such as Claude Monet and Camille Pissarro. (See Chapter 10, "Forms of Expression.")

Intensity. The saturation or strength of a color determined by the *quality* of light reflected from it. A vivid color is of high intensity, a dull color of low intensity.

Intuitive. Knowing or recognizing by an instinctive sense rather than by the application of exact rules; sensing or feeling something without a specific reason.

Light pattern. The typical relationship of light and dark shapes appearing on a form as a result of its physical character and the kind and direction of light falling upon it.

Line. A line is the path of a moving point, that is, a mark made by a tool or instrument as it is drawn across a surface. It is usually made visible by the fact that it contrasts in value with the surface on which it is drawn.

Local color. A tone which takes its color from the nature of the actual object portrayed (green grass, blue sky, etc.)

Local value. The characteristic tone quality of an area or surface which is determined by its particular pigmentation. For example, a shape painted with grey pigment will reflect only a *certain amount of light* even when that light strikes it directly.

Lyrical. A term borrowed from poetry which attempts to define a quality of a special aesthetic or sensory experience in the visual arts (as opposed to a dramatic experience, for example). A songlike outpouring of the artist's experience usually accomplished in form by graceful rhythms, light color tonalities, and spontaneous drawing or brush-work. The term *poetic* is sometimes used in place of lyrical, for the same kind of meaning.

Mass. A three-dimensional form or body which stands out from the space surrounding it because of difference in color, value, or texture.

Media, mediums. The materials and tools used by the artist to create the visual elements perceived by the viewer of the work of art.

Moments of force. Direction(s) and degree(s) of energy implied by art elements in specific pictorial situations; amounts of visual thrust produced by such matters as dimension, placement, and accent.

Motif. A visual element or a combination of elements which is repeated often enough in a composition to make it the dominating feature of the artist's expression.

Narrative art. A form of art which depends on subject matter to tell a story. At its best such art would be more concerned with aesthetic qualities than with the story; at its worst, it would be a documentary description of the facts of the story without regard for aesthetic form.

Natural texture. Texture existing as the result of natural processes.

Naturalism. The approach to art in which all forms used by the artist are essentially descriptive representation of things visually experienced. True naturalism contains no interpretation introduced by the artist for expressive purposes.

Neutralized color. A color which has been "greyed" or reduced in its intensity by mixture with a neutral or a complementary color.

Neutrals. Tones which do not reflect any single wavelength of light. Neutrals create only effects of darkness and lightness as in black, white, or grey.

Nonobjective. An approach to art in which the visual signs are entirely imaginative and do not derive from anything ever seen by the artist. The shapes, their organization, and treatment by the artist are entirely personalized and consequently not associated by the observer with any previously experienced natural form.

Objective. An impersonal statement of observed facts. In art, the exact rendering by the artist of surface characteristics without alteration or interpretation of the visual image.

Objective color. (see *Local color*)

Optical perception. A way of seeing in which the mind seems to have no other function than the natural one of providing the physical sensation of recognition by sight.

Organizational control. Specific or planned relationships of the art elements in pictorial space.

Paint Quality. The use of the medium on surfaces to give them an enrichment through textural interest. Interest is created by the ingenuity in the handling of paint for its intrinsic character.

Papier Collé. A technique of visual expression in which scraps of paper having various textures are actually pasted to the picture surface to enrich or embellish areas.

Pattern. The obvious emphasis on certain visual form relationships and certain directional movements within the visual field. It also refers to the repetition of elements or the combinations of elements in a readily recognized systematic organization.

Perception. The act of taking notice; recognition of an object, quality, or idea through the use of the physical and/or mental faculties.

Perspective. A mechanical system of creating the illusion of a three-dimensional space on a two-dimensional surface. *Linear perspective* primarily linear in treatment. *Aerial or atmospheric perspective* uses value and color modification to suggest or enhance the effect of space.

Pictorial area. The area within which the design exists; generally of measurable dimensions and bounded by mat, frame, or lines.

Picture frame. The outermost limits or the boundary of the picture plane.

Picture Plane. The actual flat surface on which the artist executes his pictorial image. In some cases it acts merely as a transparent plane of reference to establish the illusion of forms existing in a three-dimensional space.

Pigments. Coloring matter or substances used by the artist to create the effect of color on a surface.

Plane. A shape which is essentially two-dimensional in nature but whose relationships with other shapes may give an illusion of a third dimension.

Plastic. A quality which emphasizes the three-dimensional nature of shape or mass. On a two-dimensional surface, plasticity is always an illusion created by the use of the visual elements in special ways.

Positive Shapes. The enclosed areas which represent the initial selection of shapes planned by the artist. They may suggest recognizable objects or merely be planned nonrepresentational shapes.

Primary colors. The three colors in the spectrum which cannot be produced by a mixture of pigments. Red, yellow, and blue.

Primitive art. The art of people with a tribal social order or a Neolithic stage of culture. This kind of art is characterized by a heightened emphasis on form and a mysterious but vehement expression and content. A secondary meaning is found in the work of artists such as Henry Rousseau and Grandma Moses which shows a naivete of expression and form closely related to the untrained but often sensitive forms of folk-art.

Proportion. The comparison of elements one to another in terms of their properties of size, quantity, or degree of emphasis. Proportion may be expressed in terms of a definite ratio such as "twice as big," or may be more loosely indicated in such expressions as "darker than," "more neutralized" or "more important than."

Radial balance. (1) Two or more identical forces distributed around a center point to create a repetitive equilibrium. (2) Rotating forces which create a visual circular movement.

Realism. A form of expression which retains the basic impression of visual reality but deviates only enough to relate and interpret universal meanings underneath surface appearances.

Reality. (see *Visual reality*)

Rectilinear shape. A shape which may be regular or irregular in character but is basically composed of straight lines.

Relief (sculptural). Partial projection from a main mass, the degree of projection determining the type of relief; limited three-dimensional masses bound to a parent surface.

Repetition. The use of the same visual element a number of times in the same composition. It may accomplish a dominance of one visual idea, a feeling of harmonious relationship, or an obviously planned pattern.

Representation. A manner of expression by the artist in which the subject matter is naturalistically presented so that the visual elements seen by the observer are reminiscent of actual forms previously perceived.

Rhythm. A continuance or flow which is accomplished by repetition of regulated visual units. The use of measured accents.

Romanticism. A philosophical attitude toward life which may occur at any time. In art, the *romantic* form is characterized by an experimental point of view which extols spontaneity of expression, intuitive imagination, and a picturesque rather than a carefully organized, rational approach. The *Romantic* movement of 19th century artists such as Delacroix, Gericault, Turner, and others, is characterized by such an approach to form.

Saturation. (see *Intensity*)

Shades, shadows. The area of a form which is dark in value because little or no light strikes it directly.

Shape. An area having a specific character defined by an outline, or by a contrast of color, value, or texture with the surrounding area.

Simultaneity. In art, use of separate views, representing different points in time and space, brought together to create one integrated image.

Simultaneous contrast. The direct contact between two colors tends to reduce the similarities and intensify the differences of the colors.

Space. (1) The interval between pre-established points. (2) Measurable distances. (3) "Denoting time or duration." (Oxford Universal Dictionary)
Two-dimensioned. An extent (surface) possessing measurement as to length and breadth but lacking in thickness or depth.

Three-dimensioned. Possessing thickness or depth as well as length and breadth.
Four-dimensioned. Possessing time as well as thickness or depth, length, and breadth.
Decorative. In art terminology, limited to length and breadth.
Plastic. Involving length, breadth, thickness, or depth.
Infinite. A pictorial concept in which the illusion of space has the quality of endlessness found in the natural environment. The picture frame has the quality of a window through which one can see the endless recession of forms into space.
Shallow. This is sometimes called "limited depth" because the artist controls his use of the visual elements so that no point or form is so remote that it does not take its place in the pattern of the picture surface.

Spectrum. The band of colors resulting when a beam of light is broken up into its component wavelengths of hues.

Style. The specific artistic character and dominant form trends noted in art movements or during specific periods of history. It also may mean the artist's expressive use of the media to give his work an individual character.

Subject matter. This term in a descriptive style of art refers to the persons or things represented as well as the artist's experiences which serve as his inspiration. In abstract or nonobjective forms of art it merely refers to the basic character of all the visual signs employed by the artist. In this case the subject matter has little to do with anything as experienced in the natural environment.

Subjective. The personal as opposed to the impersonal; an individual attitude or bias through which the artist feels free to change or modify natural visual characteristics. In this approach, the artist is able to emphasize the emotions or feelings aroused within himself by the characteristics of the natural form.

Subjective colors. Tones which are chosen by the artists without regard to the "real" color of the object. They have nothing to do with objective reality.

Surrealism. A style of artistic expression which emphasizes fantasy and whose subjects are usually the experiences revealed by the sub-conscious mind.

Symbol. Representation of a quality or situation through the use of an intermediate agent; the word is not the thing itself but a "sign" of the thing (for example, the owl "represents" blindness); indirect understanding as opposed to direct understanding through form-meanings.

Symmetrical balance. A form of balance achieved by the use of identical compositional units on either side of a vertical axis within the confining pictorial space.

Tactile. Referring to the sense of touch.

Technique. The manner and skill with which the artist employs his tools and materials to achieve a predetermined expressive effect. The ways of using the media can have an effect on the aesthetic quality of the artist's total concept.

Tenebrism. A style of painting which exaggerates or emphasizes the effects of chiaroscuro. Larger amounts of dark value are placed close to smaller areas of highly contrasting lights in order to concentrate the attention on certain important features.

Tension (pictorial). Dynamic interrelationships of force as manifested by the moments of force inherent in art elements; semi-architectural stresses affecting balance.

Texture. The surface feel of an object or the representation of surface character. Texture is the actual and "visual feel" of surface areas as they are arranged and altered by man or nature.
Actual. A surface which stimulates a tactile response when actually touched.
Simulated. A representation of an actual texture created by a careful copying of the light and dark pattern characteristic of its surface.
Invented. Two-dimensional patterns sometimes derived from actual textures, frequently varied to fit pictorial needs, and often freely created without reference to any item.

Tonality. An orderly planning in terms of selection and arrangement of color schemes or color combinations. It would concern itself not only with hue, but also with value and intensity relationships.

Tone. The character of color or value of a surface determined by the amount or quality of light reflected from it. The kind of light reflected may be determined by the character of the medium which has been applied to the surface.

Trompe l'oeil. A painting technique involving the copying of nature with such exactitude that the painted objects may be mistaken for the actual forms depicted.

Unity. The whole or total effect of a work of art which results from the combination of all of its component parts.

Value. (1) The tone quality of lightness or darkness given to a surface or an area by the *amount of light* reflected from it. (2) (color) The characteristic of a color in terms of lightness and darkness. This is determined by the amount or quantity of light reflected by a color.

Value Pattern. The total effect of the relationships of light and dark given to areas within the pictorial field.
(1) *Two-dimensional.* Value relationships in which the changes of light and dark seem to occur only on the surface of the picture plane.
(2) *Three-dimensional.* The value relationships which are planned to create an illusion of objects existing in depth back of the picture plane.

Visual reality. The objective (insofar as that is possible) optical image; obvious appearances; naturalism in the sense of the physically observed.

Volume. A shape having three dimensions or one which gives the illusion of solidity or mass.

Wash. A transparent layer or coating of color applied to a surface allowing underlying lines, shapes, or colors to show through. Any transparent medium may be lightly applied to previously painted shapes or areas in order to modify their appearance without completely hiding or covering them.

APPENDIX II: CHRONOLOGICAL OUTLINE OF WESTERN ART

200,000 B.C.	PREHISTORIC ART.	PALEOLITHIC — Old Stone Age.	
		Flint-tool industries.	
25,000 B.C.		Art Beginnings — cave painting, etc.	
10,000 B.C.		NEOLITHIC — New Stone Age.	
		Beginning of architecture, pottery, weaving.	
4000 B.C.	ANCIENT ART.	EGYPTIAN — Old Kingdom.	
3000 B.C.		MIDDLE EAST — Sumerian Babylonian.	
2800 B.C.		AEGEAN ART — Cretan (Minoan I).	
2200 B.C.		Cretan (Minoan II).	
2100 B.C.		EGYPTIAN — Mid-Kingdom.	
1800 B.C.		AEGEAN ART — Mycenaen Age (in Greece).	
1700 B.C.		AEGEAN ART — Cretan (Minoan III).	
		MIDDLE EAST — Assyrian.	
1580 B.C.		EGYPTIAN — New Empire.	
1200 B.C.			
1100 B.C.		AEGEAN ART — Homeric Age.	ETRUSCAN ART, Italy.
1090 B.C.		EGYPTIAN — Decadence and foreign influences.	
750 B.C.		GREEK ART — Archaic Age.	ETRUSCO-ROMAN, Italy
606 B.C.		MIDDLE EAST — Chaldean — Babylonian	
530 B.C.		MIDDLE EAST — Persian (to ca.225 B.C.)	
470 B.C.		GREEK ART — *Classical Age.*	
338 B.C.		GREEK ART — Hellenistic Age.	
332 B.C.		Egypt. — Greeco — Egyptian or Ptolemaic.	
280 B.C.			Graeco-ROMAN.
146 B.C.		Greece — Roman domination.	ROMAN.
30 B.C.		Egypt. — Roman domination.	
300 A.D.	MEDIEVAL ART.	EARLY CHRISTIAN Art in Italy.	
330 A.D.		EARLY BYZANTINE ART in Mid-East, Egypt (Coptic)	
550 A.D.		MOHAMMEDAN or ISLAMIC ART, No. Africa, So. Spain (Moorish art).	
768 A.D.		Carolingian Art, France, Germany, No. Italy.	
800 A.D.		DEVELOPED BYZANTINE ART, Mid-East, Greece, Russia, parts of Italy (Ravenna, Rome) (to 1453).	
		Migratory, barbarian (Vikings; Huns, Goths) and Early Christian art in Western Europe.	
1000 A.D.		ROMANESQUE (Roman-like, or modified Roman art in France, England, No. Spain, Italy, and Germany.)	
1150 A.D.		GOTHIC ART in Europe.	
1300 A.D.	RENAISSANCE ART.	Proto-RENAISSANCE, Italy, Giotto, Duccio.	
1400 A.D.		EARLY — Masaccio, Donatello, Francesca, Leonardo, etc.	
		Renaissance in West modified by vestiges of Medievalism. Van Eycks, Weyden, Van der Goes.	
1500 A.D.		HIGH REN. — Michelangelo, Raphael, Titian, Tintoretto, W. Europe influenced by Italy.	
1520 A.D.		Mannerism and Early Baroque, Italy.	

1600 A.D.   BAROQUE ART.   BAROQUE ART in Europe. Age of Rubens, Rembrandt, Velasquez, etc. Early
                                  Colonial art, America.
1700 A.D.   ROCOCO ART (primarily French, but spreads somewhat to other countries
                                  of Europe). Colonial art in the Americas.

1800 A.D.   MODERN ART.   Neo-Classicism — David, Ingres.
1820   Romanticism — Gericault — Delacroix, Turner.
1850   French centered Realism and Naturalism — Daumier, Courbet, Manet. movements. Impressionism —
1870   Monet, Pissarro, Renoir
1880   Post-Impressionism — Cezanne, Seurat, Van Gogh, Gauguin.

1900 A.D.   20th CENTURY MOVEMENTS
1901   EXPRESSIONISM. Picasso, Blue, Rose, Negro periods.
1905   *Les Fauves,* France.   ⌐ *Die Brucke* (Bridge), Germany.
                                 Matisse, Rouault, Vlaminck,   Nolde, Kirchner, Mueller, Kokoschka.
                                 Derain.
1906   ABSTRACT ART.
                                 Cubism, Picasso, Braque, Leger.
                                 Futurism, Italy.

1910   FANTASY in ART.   Boccioni, Balla, Severini,, Car-
              Chirico, Chagall   ra.
                 Klee, Rousseau   *Abstraction* and *Non-Objective*   ⊣ *Der Blaue Reiters* (Blue Riders) Ger-
1911   art.   many. Marc, Kandinsky, Klee, Jaw-
                                    Russia — Larionev, Malevich,   lenski, Macke.
                                     Gabo.
                                    Germany — Kandinsky, Klee,
                                     Albers.
                                    France — Delaunay
                                    Holland — Mondrian, Van
                                     Doesburg, Van Tongerloo.
                                    England — Ben Nicholson
                                    U.S.A. — Feininger, Stella,
                                     O'Keefe, Davis, Demuth,
                                     Knaths, Pereira.

1916   *Dadaism-Tzara,*
              Duchamp, Arp,
              Ernst, Picabia
1924   *Orthodox Surrealism*
              Ernst, Tanguy, Dali

1925   — *Surreal-Abstraction*   ⊢ *Die Neue Saachlichkeit* (The New Ob-
                                 Miro, Masson, Tamayo,   jectivity) Grosz, Dix.
                                 Matts, Baziotes, Tobey.
1930   Gorky, Graves.
                                                                             ⌐ *Recent Expressionists* Weber, Munch,
                                                                               Soutine, Beckmann, Orozco, Shahn,
                                                                               Levine, Avery, Kuhn, Buffet, Balthus.

1945   —— *Abstract Expressionism* (Begins in U.S.A.)
                                        Gorky, Hoffman, Motherwell, Pollock, De Koon-
                                        ing, Brooks. (Parallel movements in Europe)

1960   *Pop Art*   —— *Op Art*
              Warhol, Lichtenstein,   Vasarely, Albers
              Dine, Oldenburg,   Anuszkiewicz, Ortmann,
              Indiana, Thiebaud   Agam, Riley

APPENDIX III: BIBLIOGRAPHY

Barnhart, Clarence L., *American College Dictionary,* 3rd ed., Random House, Inc., New York, 1949.

Barr, Alfred H. Jr., *Painting and Sculpture in The Museum of Modern Art,* Simon and Schuster, Inc., New York, 1946.

Bethers, Ray, *Composition in Pictures,* 2nd ed., Pitman Publishing Corp., New York, London, 1956.

Canaday, John, *Mainstreams of Modern Art,* Henry Holt & Co., Inc., New York, 1959.

Cheney, Sheldon, *Expressionism in Art,* Liveright Publishing Co., New York, 1934.

Emerson, Sybil, *Design: A Creative Approach,* International Textbook Co., Scranton, 1953.

Gardner, Helen, *Art Through the Ages,* 2nd ed. rev., Harcourt, Brace & Co., Inc., New York, 1936.

Kepes, Gyorgy, *Language of Vision,* Paul Theobald & Co., Chicago, 1951.

Longman, Lester, *History and Appreciation of Art,* Wm. C. Brown and Co., Dubuque, Iowa, 1949.

Mather, Frank J., *Concerning Beauty,* Princeton University Press, New Jersey, 1935.

McCurdy, Charles, editor, *Modern Art: A Pictorial Anthology,* Macmillian Co., New York, 1958.

Moholy-Nagy, L., *Vision in Motion,* 5th ed., Paul Theobald & Co., Chicago, 1956.

Munro, Thomas, *Great Pictures of Europe,* Tudor Publishing Co., New York, 1934.

Onions, C. T., editor, *The Oxford Universal Dictionary,* 3rd ed., Oxford, Clarendon Press, London, 1955.

Rasmusen, Henry N., *Art Structure,* McGraw-Hill Book Co., New York, Toronto, London, 1950.

Runes, Dagobert D. and Schrickel, Harry G., *Encyclopedia of the Arts,* Philosophical Library, New York, 1946.

Scott, Robert G., *Design Fundamentals,* McGraw-Hill Book Book Co., New York, Toronto, London, 1951.

Seltman, Charles, *Approach to Greek Art,* The Studio Publications, London, New York, 1948.

Vincent, Jean Anne, *History of Art,* College Outline Series #95, Barnes & Noble, Inc., New York, 1955.

Webster, N. Merriam, *Webster's Collegiate Dictionary,* 5th ed., G. & C. Merriam Co., Springfield, Mass., 1941.

Wickiser, Ralph L., *An Introduction to Art Activities,* Henry Holt & Co., New York, 1947.

INDEX